D1422307

The relevance of celibacy in the church's life can only be appreciated spiritually. All other attempts to explain it are inevitably inadequate. Gabriel Harty writes about the meaning of celibacy in a profoundly spiritual – and sometimes mystical – way. He stresses that a wholesome understanding of celibacy necessarily associates it with every aspect of daily living. His *Letters to the Beloved* offers a challenging reflection on the gift of celibacy to the church, especially at a time when so many people dismiss its importance and advocate its abolition.

John Littleton
President, National Conference of Priests of Ireland

Maire Treasa.

May the Lord make his Face to shine upon you + be gracious to you

Gabriel Harty cp
30·1·07

Gabriel Harty OP

A Celibate Way of Loving

LETTERS TO THE BELOVED

the columba press

First published in 2005 by
ᴄhe coluᴍʙᴀ pʀess
55A Spruce Avenue, Stillorgan Industrial Park,
Blackrock, Co Dublin

Cover by Bill Bolger
Origination by The Columba Press
Printed in Ireland by Betaprint, Dublin

ISBN 1 85607 504 4

Table of Contents

Personal Note

For over fifty years, I have been preaching the Rosary. It may seem strange that the present work should be the outcome of that ministry.

Let me explain: the Rosary became popular as a means of overcoming the strange puritanical and divisive heresy of the Catharists, or Albigensians. This group maintained that the material world was of an evil source. The spirit which was of God could not possibly be held in a house of flesh.

This led to a denial of the Incarnation. The Catharists could not embrace the notion of the Word made flesh, born of the Virgin Mary. Neither could they accept the goodness of the man/woman relationship in marriage. Human sexuality was a dark forest where one got lost.

To the rescue came Francis of Assisi, singing of the goodness of creation, of Brother Sun and Sister Moon. St Dominic proclaimed the dignity of woman and the glory of human nature in the light of Jesus, born of the Virgin Mary.

My hope is that these letters of a celibate who has sought to love, may be of some help to those who still wander in the dark forest of their sexuality. Keep a green bough in your heart, and God will send a singing bird.

Gabriel Harty OP

Blessed Jordan of Saxony,
Second Master General of the Dominican Order

This book has been inspired by the letters of Blessed Jordan of Saxony, written to his beloved friend Diana d'Andalo. I quote from the edition of Gerald Vann's work entitled, *To Heaven with Diana:*

> 'Beloved, since I cannot see you with my bodily eyes, nor be consoled by your presence as often as you would wish and I would wish, it is at least to me some appeasment of my heart's longing, when I can visit you by means of my letters. Within our hearts is the ardour of our love in the Lord, whereby you speak to me and I do continuously in those wordless outpourings of love which no tongue can express nor letter contain.
>
> O Diana, you weep because it is not given you to see me continually. When I have to part from you, I do so with a heavy heart ...
>
> Am I not yours, yours when I am far away, yours in prayer, your in merit, yours too I hope in the eternal reward? Were I to die, you would not be losing me: you would be sending me before you to those shining dwellings, that abiding there, I might pray for you to the Father, and so be of greater use to you there, living with the Lord, than here in this world, where I die all the day long. Farewell. Christ Jesus, be with you.'

Introducing the Beloved

John waited each evening before the TV until the presenter looked out and smiled and said, 'Goodnight'. He could then take his cocoa and retire to sleep-land. But then one night, he could only toss and tumble in the bed. Something had gone dreadfully wrong. The lovely lady on the TV had smiled as usual, but instead of saying 'Goodnight', she said, 'Goodnight everybody'! It was the end of the dream. He had thought he was the one and only.

I had a similar experience as a young priest. The Mother Prioress had been so kind and had always spoken to me as if I were special. Then one day as I cycled past the hall door, I saw her wish a visitor bye-bye. I knew from the way she held his hand and looked straight into his face, that I had at least one other rival. It was only years later, when I knew her better, that I understood something of the particularity that is built into the universal divine love.

Frank Duff, the founder of the Legion of Mary, had this same character about him. I frequently met him at the Legion Headquarters from which he surveyed the whole wide mission-world. With this hinterland in the caverns of his mind, he would treat you as if you were the only one that counted. He gave you the full range of his attention, and all the time you wanted. When he died you found out that there were hundreds who could testify to the same experience.

This is by way of introducing you to my Beloved. She is one and she is one in a thousand. She is yesterday and today and to-morrow.

She is single and celibate, she is married and has a family of her own. She lives in a certain place and yet only exists in mind and heart. She is personally and intimately known, and yet is summoned up from dreams and desires. She is one, and she is everyone.

St Francis de Sales favoured this way of writing his *Treatise on The Love of God*. While his teaching is profound and sometimes difficult to wade through, you sense that there is a wealth of personal experience here, when he every now and then addresses himself to his friend, Theotimus, as he had already addressed each chapter of his *Introduction to The Devout Life* to Philothea.

When the Angel Gabriel came to Mary, he came at the same time to the whole waiting world with the gift of the Word made flesh. 'Rejoice, the Lord is with you.' Mary was our stand-in, the representative of all human nature. The words addressed to her, we can take to ourselves. Mary is the icon in which creation is mirrored and all things are groaning with expectation of the saving Lord. Mary is the image of the whole church, and what is said of her and to her, is said to one and all.

And so, beloved, these letters, while addressed to all, are written to you, as if you were the one and only.

An Instrument of my Love

Beloved,

You tell me how it seemed as if the Lord was saying to you: 'I will make you an instrument of my love.'

There lies a precious secret. We are not prime agents of love. For love is a fire that comes from the high hills of heaven, and which we must handle with respect and reverence. Before we run to meet it, we may have to sit in silence, and at times wander in the woodlands and by-ways waiting and watching.

Frail and fickle instruments that we are, we often rush into love, or wake it before its time. To be open to such instrumentality demands humility. Humble people will not attribute the fruit of love to themselves. They will not rob God of his glory. Abandoning themselves into his loving hands, they become mighty instruments of his divine plans and purposes.

Natural love becomes instrumental to the overarching dynamic of divine love. In the measure that it falls short of this end, love lies bleeding and fails to reach its destiny. Christ's prayer was that we might share in his very own love for the Father: 'I have made your name known to them ... that the love with which you loved me, may be in them.' Pray, beloved, that you may continue to hear love's call and trust that it leads you true.

Many have been led to suppress their affectivity and enthusiasm even with regard to pretty basic things like thanking their host for a good meal or expressing delight in the appearance or dress of another, thinking this might be the start of some slippery slope.

A certain devout priest, who has since gone on to be a renowned spiritual director, was taken aback when a good lady said to him: 'God loves you and I do too. It is not difficult to love you.' The man had been brought up to bury his own self-esteem and ward off any manifestation of affection. He was not for being loved, any more than he was for loving.

Lust can masquerade as love, and fallen nature can easily lead one astray. But for those who have found Jesus, the Word made flesh, and whose own flesh has been refined by their union with him, there is a new transforming creation. St Paul remarks that 'all we, beholding the glory of the Lord, are being transformed into his likeness, from one degree of glory to another.' (2 Cor: 3:18)

True love is thus being continually transfigured and ever on the move. This is not to be understood as a flitting from one situation to another, but rather in the sense of growing from the flickering glow of candlelight to the living flame of divine passion. This love has a mothering as well as a spousal quality, as it gives birth to ever-deeper levels of understanding and consideration for others. It is a giving love and while deeply enjoyable, is never self-centred.

'Love is always patient and kind. It is never jealous … rude or selfish.' If only we could burn those golden words of St Paul into our souls, what a wonderful world this would be. Love like this may travel in a desert of pain and desolation but through this desert it is accompanied by the twin companions of faith and hope, that bear it on their arms.

Bearing the wounds of love the faith-filled soul continues to walk with head held high into the land of promise. Christ came to teach us this way of wounded love. For many years I shared with some beautiful people who called themselves *The Rosary Group for the Little Wounded Ones*. After each decade they prayed like this:

God our Father, we press our open wounds
To the precious wounds of Jesus, your Son,
That your will and ours be one.
Through these shared wounds, may we be healed
And bring your healing love to others,
That all may be enriched, in the fullness of love
through Jesus, the Divine Humanity.

Moaning and Groaning over Celibacy

Beloved,

There is really no reason to moan and groan over celibacy as if it were a stranglehold on your capacity to love. The truth of the matter is that the celibate who has learned to discipline the motions of the body and bring them into harmony with the movement of the Holy Spirit, is on the high road to life in its fullness. I write not of an emasculated kind of loving, but of an authentic and splendidly human way of giving and receiving love. The idea that celibates must cut out their sexuality is not the truth. They are to be totally fulfilled according to the measure of their vocation, as they allow the kindly light of God's love to lead them through the darkness. We must not, however, think in merely human and psychological terms. God does not allow us to share with another, until they are first exclusively his.

I have heard of celibate people who come home to what they call an empty house, with no one to greet them and nothing to do, but reach for the bottle and drown their sorrow. I can't see that as part of the divine plan. The Bible has, as one of its most basic texts, that it is not good for man to be alone. Male and female they have been made, to express the divine image which is their destiny.

The sacred text does not say that all are called to physical sexual intercourse. It does, however, state that all are made for relationship and that essential relationship is between male and female. In biblical terms, no one is meant to live in total isolation or to be bound up in a merely one sex relationship.

Incidentally, this is not just a problem that faces Catholic priests and religious. What about the countless numbers of young people who face into long stages of third level education? Many of these are into their late twenties or even thirty before they can contemplate marriage and physical sexual intercourse. How are they to handle their love-lives and their relationships?

What have we to offer them? The church does not approve of condoms and other such related methods of contraception. The plain fact is that we are asking people to remain celibate for long sustained periods and offering them no real help. We need to widen the horizons of celibacy and show it for what it is, a special way of loving and not just a legal restriction.

Writing in *The Furrow*, a magazine for the Irish clergy, a lay woman, Ben Kimmerling stated that 'even those who love partners, with sexual-genital love, are also called to love those who are not partners, in a celibate way ... Jesus demonstrated the human capacity for celibate love and the inner freedom to love many people which celibacy confers … He proved that in spite of our sexual relationships, it is possible for men and women to love another in a celibate way … He proved too, that it is possible to love, equally and tenderly, more than one person of the opposite sex at the same time. He proved that while retaining all the elements of particularity, it is possible for a group of people to create a climate, a communion of love.'

The very groaning of a celibate clergy testifies to the fact that they have not found a satisfactory means of living their own solitary life. It might help if we widen the horizon of celibacy to see it not so much as a restricted territory, but as a wide terrain where many are called to walk with joyful expectancy and splendid possibility.

Men, it is true, experience much of their sexual satisfaction to be associated with their genitality and find that it is often more a burden than a comfort. Those who avoid female company as a protection against temptation may only store up more trouble. Repression and denial are of little help and may indeed breed bitterness and frustration down the line.

Beloved, you have shown me that the company of a good woman offers hope of a higher way. Your genuine love has taught me that there is a world of difference between love and lust. You treasure intimacy, tenderness, understanding, and offer a vision of relationship that is often unknown to mere males. Now I know that the groans of the celibate male can be sweetened by the gentle calling of the good woman who is walking the ways of authentic human loving. Most men seem to need the help of woman in order to find their way through the dark forest of human sexuality.

We need to get out of the fantasy world in which we can get lost. The great remedy for fantasy is reality. Playing mind-games with fantasy men and women leads to a fool's paradise. With a real man or woman we are challenged to move up a gear into the world of persons. No longer is the other a mere object of pleasure, but a full person to be lived with and to be loved with all that we are, and all that we have.

I'll end this letter, beloved, by inviting you to search the gospel of St John, the beloved disciple, for that short simple line ... 'now Jesus loved Martha ...'

PS:
I've just come across this note from *The Legend of Perugia*:

During the sickness of St Clare, which occurred in the last week of St Francis's life, she was afraid that she herself might die and thus be unable to have a last glimpse of her precious friend. Out of compassion, Francis dictated a special blessing for her and her sisters.

'The blessing I often pray is not just for yourself, as I do not see myself standing over you, but rather kneeling beside you.

I ask dear Jesus to draw us ever more into the recesses of his heart, and make us one in his love and use us as an intrument of his healing love for others.'

Love is a Decision

Beloved,

My cousin, Ann, was going on a motor-bike holiday with her boy-friend and her mother was a bit anxious about how things would work out. 'You're going to be thrown together a lot,' she said. 'I hope you know what you are doing and that you'll be safe.' 'Don't worry about us Mum. We'll be wearing helmets!'

Helmets are fine when you get thrown off the bike. But you need more than that to get through the day, not to talk of the night, which brings us back to the young and their sexuality. They are called to celibacy just as much as the priest and the nun.

Teenage might be considered as a noviceship for marriage. If it is left to drift and to drag along without direction, it can be a terrible waste of precious time. Whatever our age, we all need to appreciate that love is not just a bodily drive. It is a dynamic of the whole personality, embracing intellect, will, emotion, sentiment, and the whole gamut of the senses. The trouble is that for the growing, impulsive stage of life, the lower bodily organs (if we may call them that), can easily outrun the higher ranges of flesh and spirit.

I first heard at a Marriage Encounter weekend, that *Love is a decision*. It may not be a complete definition, but it does touch on an aspect that can raise one to a new and challenging level of loving. We have to rest in the mind and endeavour to cultivate sureness of intellect and firmness of will, so as to come to an intelligent decision. Moreover, this is not a once-off thing. Love has to be a daily decision. This can help to lessen the overburden of sensual satisfaction that makes such demands on youth.

St Paul warns about the struggle that goes on between flesh and spirit, but goes on to talk about the reconciliation that must come about between these warring elements in the human personality. He puts us in touch with Jesus as the Reconciler. When he is recognised as Lord, and we learn to surrender to his Lordship, there comes about a sweetness and a harmony that permeates all creation.

The priest who acts in the name of the great Reconciler at the offering of the Mass prays thus:

> Blessed are you Lord, God of all creation. Through your goodness, we have this bread and wine. May they become for us food and drink for eternal life.

If the elements of bread and wine can be transformed and become divinised, through the power of God, what cannot the Lord of Creation do with the elements of the human personality?

To Heaven with Diana

Beloved,

You've often spoken of the unclaimed treasures that come to your door: the unmarried, yet loveable, and eager to love. They are celibate but ready for relationship. They have labelled themselves as *on the shelf!*

I've news for you. There have been saints who were deeply in love while remaining celibate. They were genuinely holy people and most active in the proclamation of the gospel. They were delightfully human and attractive men and women. They eagerly sought out each other's company and when they were apart, they were distressed.

One outstanding pair are members of my own Dominican Order, Jordan of Saxony and Diana d'Andalo, both acknowledged Blesseds of the Catholic Church. There are two books about their beautiful loving relationship which speak for themselves. One entitled *To Heaven with Diana*, is the work of the eminent Dominican priest, Gerald Vann, the other is entitled *Love among the Saints*, a translation by Kathleen Pond.

Jordan, a man of manifold gifts, became the immediate successor of St Dominic and like him was frequently on the roads. His colleagues recognised him as especially gentle or sweet natured, beloved of God, and kind towards all. He was particularly concerned that women would be a loving prayerful support to the brethren of the Order. From his travels he wrote to Diana, and it would appear that his many concerns for others found a focus in the deep affection and delight he experienced with her. As a husband goes out to work from the loving company of his wife, abides in spirit there throughout the day, and returns home at evening, so Jordan was supported in the rigours of his apostolic work by the eager loving longing heart of Diana.

When unable to be together, Jordan would express his feelings by letter. No doubt, Diana replied in similar fashion, perhaps even more ardently. This is clear from a letter of his, which says: 'I am convinced that I do not respond adequately to your love. You love me more fully than I love you. However, I am distressed that you are so afflicted in body and in mind, by reason of this love of yours which is so precious to me.'

Six years later his own weak love seems to have flowered and he writes: 'When I have to part from you, it is with a heavy heart. Still you add to my sorrow when I see you so saddened by our separation which afflicts us both ...'

No doubt Jordan and Diana had their sights on the delights of heaven, but that did not prevent them enjoying the good things of creation on this earth. They lived well in both worlds, totally divinised by grace and totally grounded in the reality of the man-woman image in which they were made. At Christmas, Jordan wrote to his beloved of the Word made flesh in Jesus, but at the same time sent her what he termed 'the little word of his own great love.'

This love relationship would go on even after death, for he once wrote: 'You are engraven on my heart. I realise that you love me from the depths of your soul. I am incapable of forgetting you. You are constantly in my thoughts ... May the Consoler and Paraclete, the Spirit of truth, possess and comfort your heart and grant us to be with one another forever in the heavenly Jerusalem through the grace of our Lord Jesus Christ.'

Beloved, I cannot better express my longing to be with yourself, for time and for eternity. You are my heaven on earth and how much more wonderful it shall be in that heaven that awaits us. Let's not think, or say, or do anything, that might hinder this full flowering of love.

PS. Have you seen the extraordinary letters, the Little Flower wrote to her priest-friend, Fr Maurice?

They are a testimony to the gift of friendship among the saints. The Carmelite nun loved this priest in a way that was at once truly human and divine, with a blessing that reached from earth to heaven. She said: 'What matters life or death to me. How unhappy I shall be in heaven if I cannot do little favours for those whom I love.'

St Francis de Sales and Jane de Chantal

Beloved,

Your words about Mother Teresa prompt me to send you this piece which I am working on at present. I'm well aware of the great universal love of Mother Teresa and how she embraced all the poor she found on the streets of Calcutta. We too must have something of that concern in our outreach. We have to be all things to all people.

But where you and I are concerned, beloved, there is something more, something unique. You are not just one of many. You are my chosen one, the beloved. After all didn't the Father speak words like these from the heights of heaven at the Baptism of Jesus, and again at the Transfiguration: 'This is my Beloved, the Chosen one.'

The love that compelled Blessed Jordan to write so ardently to Blessed Diana would be meaningless and mockery if she were not special and chosen in his eyes.

St Francis de Sales had a love of similar nature for the holy nun, Jane de Chantal. A card from him, found among the possessions of Jane after her death, showed how the love he had for her had woven its way into his spiritual life. It read: 'When I was at Mass this morning, the Lord revealed to me that the love I have for you was his gift and that I was to cherish and honour you always.'

An English writer, commenting on the life of Francis de Sales, seemed quite confused when she came to deal with the letters he had written to St Jane. They were so expressly tender and intimate that she tried to excuse them or explain them away by saying that they were typical of the excessive poetic charm of the French language of the time. No doubt many would think the same. I believe that this freedom of expression, and the style of relationship it implies, is not for beginners in the life of the spirit. It is for those who have schooled themselves in the discipline of temperance and self-denial over the years. Love born out of circumstances like this, is in no way narrow or closed in on itself. It spills over in lavish fruitfulness in the community and in the apostolic work of the lover.

Karl Rahner SJ wrote moving letters of love up to five times a week to the poet Luise Rinser. He told her of the delight and encouragement she had afforded him when he had to deal with much opposition to his work. As a theologian, rooted in the teaching of St Paul, Rahner would have realised that the love he experienced was a God-given charismatic gift deriving out of divine love. As such, it was not simply a personal enrichment, but an instrument of growth for the whole community and was to be exercised in the service of all.

Only when Jesus has been enthroned in the heart of the Christian soul, can love be allowed to run freely into the heart of another in this kind of friendship. Selfishness has to be driven out and the good of the other must be sought at all times. There is here, an element of mothering love. St Paul writes of it in his first letter to the Thessalonians:

Like a mother feeding and looking after her children, we felt so devoted and protective towards you, and had come to love you so much, that we were eager to hand over to you not only the Good News but our whole lives as well.

Preachers of the gospel are not always that eager to hand over their lives to the congregation that fills the seats before them. Maybe, they can begin with one, and in and through that one, reach out to others.

Beloved, it is not easy to be intimate and utterly tender with a large convention or congregation. And so, I want you to know that when I go to such gatherings, or when I write, I act rather like my master, Blessed Jordan. As Diana was constantly in his mind and heart, I carry you in my heart, and in the love I bear you, reach out to all. The love I bear you while unique, has about it a universal dynamic that breathes forth the love of Jesus and burns with the fire of the Holy Spirit.

My True Love hath my heart

Beloved,

Let me share with you this poem by Sir Philip Sidney. The Catholic Church must have seen a definite spiritual significance in it, for it has been inserted into the collection of sacred verse for the Divine Office.

> My true love hath my heart and I have his,
> By just exchange one for another given;
> I hold his dear, and mine he cannot miss,
> There never was a better bargain driven.
> My true love hath my heart and I have his.
>
> His heart in me keeps him and me in one,
> My heart in him his thoughts and senses guides;
> He loves my heart, for once it was his own,
> I cherish his, because in me it bides.
> My true love hath my heart and I have his.

Literature is full of thought of this kind which sees intimate human relationship as an exchange of hearts, an exchange that brings not just union, but unity. Francis de Sales constantly speaks of this unity to his Beloved Jane: 'Our union, our single heart, the one soul of our own life and the one life of our soul. God has established for us a most invariable and indissoluble unity. May he be eternally blessed. I shall not speak to you of the greatness of my heart in your regard, but I shall tell you that it dwells far above every comparison. This affection is whiter than snow, purer than the sun. Lord, God what a consolation it will be for us in heaven to love each other in that full sea of divine love.'

Beloved, I realise that this unity cannot easily rest long on this whiter than snow level. It is well to remember that we are talking here of those who have already gone apart to walk alone with the Lord of all hearts. To be worthy of heaven, any human exchange of hearts must first find its rest in the Sacred Heart of Jesus.

One thinks of Catherine of Siena who was meditating on the Psalm, *Create in me a clean heart, O Lord, and renew a right spirit in me*. It seemed that Jesus appeared to her, and opening her side, took out her heart and carried it away. Two days later, Our Lord appeared again bearing in his hand a heart that cast forth bright rays of fire. Opening her side once more, he placed this heart there, saying, 'I took your heart. Now I give you mine, to serve in its place.' She no longer prayed as formerly, 'My God, I give you my heart,' but rather, 'My God, I give you, your heart.'

It seemed to her that her own heart had entered into the side of Jesus, to be one with his. 'I am no longer the same,' she remarked to her confessor, 'The fire of love which burns in my soul is so great, no earthly fire could compare with it.'

No need, however, to think that the fire of divine love will damp down the love I have in my heart for you, beloved. Grace does not destroy nature. It only enhances it.

The Treatise on the Love of God

Beloved,

The wonder of the love I have for you, is part of the wonder that pervades the whole of creation. At the dawn of all things, God saw that all was good that came from his hand. It might be more accurate to say that all was good because it came from his heart. When you and I love others, it is because they already exist. We stumble upon them and reach out to them in love.

Not so, with the Creator! Before creation, there is nothing out there already for him to stumble upon. It is his infinite love that brings things and persons into being. God's love is the creative dynamic force that breathes creatures into existence. I can admire the loveliness of a tree, but only God can make a tree. And only God can make a person as lovely as you are, beloved. That's why I love you in God and God in you.

St Francis de Sales, throughout *The Treatise on the love of God* lingers over the beauty and the harmony of nature. He writes: 'God, the Sovereign beauty, is the author of beautiful harmony and of the charm we find in all things.' The saint would take his friends for a walk through the fine garden along the beautiful lake of Annecy and delight in sharing the splendour of nature's bounty with them. Watching the water fountains, he would remark: 'When will fountains of living waters spring up in our hearts.'

For Francis, the human heart and all its longings fitted in to this harmony of creation which the Lord saw as good. This helps one to understand the deep torrent of love he experienced for St Jane de Chantal. He writes to her: 'Each affection has its particular difference from all others. That which I have for you has a certain special quality which consoles me infinitely. To express it freely, is extremely profitable for me.'

This expression of love is no mere human passion or fleshly desire. Francis sees it as a Godly command, a duty laid upon him. 'My affection is not satisfied, for it is insatiable in its desire to render to my God the duty I have towards you ... Every day I am more confirmed in the belief that it is God who imposes this duty upon me. That is why I cherish it so incomparably.'

There was mutuality of giving and receiving in this relationship that proved a very great help in producing the work *Treatise on the Love of God*. Francis mentions 'the note I have received from you and keep and examine carefully. Our alliance is completely founded in God. It will last for all eternity, thanks to the mercy of him who is its author.'

He loved her with a love which was part of the harmony of all creation, yet did not terminate there. As long as love is limited by nature, it will have only a limited orbit, a goodness and beauty that will wither and fade. But when exposed to the sun of God's glory and sanctified by his Spirit, it will flourish and be resplendent with a lustre that never fades.

That, beloved, is why we cannot rest overlong in a joy that is merely of this world. While our feet are rooted in the dust of earth, the eyes of the spirit are always on the hills of heaven.

Kierkegaard and Regina

Beloved,

Kierkegaard, the Danish philosopher and theologian, has some things to say about love which give a profound insight into the Christian view of love and marriage. The man himself came from an unhappy family background, having lost his mother and five siblings within two years. At the age of twenty-two he discovered that his father had seduced his mother before marrying her, something that left him so disturbed that he referred to it as *the great earthquake*.

In 1840 Kierkegaard became engaged to the seventeen-year-old Regina Olsen, but broke off the engagement after a year. He was so haunted by this, that in his writings he frequently tried to justify his behaviour. In his work, *Fear and Trembling*, he suggested that he had to sacrifice his own beloved, Regina, for religious reasons, just as Abraham had to be willing to sacrifice his son Isaac because of a divine command.

In *Works of Love*, he wrote:

No love and no expression of love may, in the merely human and worldly sense, be deprived of a relationship to God. Love is a passionate emotion, but in this emotion, even before he enters into a relation with the object of his love, the man must first enter into a relationship with God, and thereby realise the claim that love is the fulfilment of the law. As soon as one leaves out the God-relationship, the questions at issue become merely human determinations.

The one who in love belongs to a woman, will first and foremost belong to God. He will not seek first to please his wife, but will first endeavour to make his love pleasing unto God. It is not the wife who will teach her husband how he ought to love her, or the husband the wife, or the friend the friend. It is God who will teach every individual how he ought to love. When the God-relationship determines what love is, then love is kept from pausing in any self-deception or illusion.

Beloved, whether we be married or single, we are all called to love and to relationship. Love is no doddle, as I once thought it would be. There is a price to pay for living in love, and a very high price to pay for climbing into God's love.

'A new commandment I give you,' said Jesus, 'that you love one another.' Why new? Because the love that is Christian stretches out it's arms, not only to embrace the other but to say , 'this is my body given up for you ... my blood shed for you.' Beloved, even as we embrace, let us keep our eyes on Jesus who having loved his own, loved them even unto death. William Blake wrote:

> Love seeketh not itself to please
> Nor for itself hath care.
> But for another gives its ease
> And builds a heaven in hell's despair.

The many-splendoured range of sexuality

Beloved,

As you know, I have just finished a six week course entitled *Counselling in matters of human sexuality*. It proved fascinating to find that periods of abstinence were being proposed to married couples as a way of dealing with their relational problems. There were a few nuns and priests present, and the whole procedure stunned us into a realisation that celibacy was not such a burden as we sometimes supposed it to be.

The lecturer said quite bluntly that marriage often placed too much weight on physical intercourse. Relying on a passing and immediate quick-fix operation was a cheap way of building a marriage. For the woman at least, and often for the man, it was like the child at the circus, who cried, 'Is this all there is?' Marriage can become a bit of a circus, subject to the law of diminishing returns. 'What is needed,' said the lecturer, 'is the discovery of the many-splendoured range of sexuality.'

Those with problem marriages were told to abstain from physical intercourse for a period of weeks. In the first week, they were simply to sit close and observe each other in love. Eye contact was to be stage one. The second week, they could hold hands and reveal their hearts and minds. In the third week, they could kiss and embrace. So the stages developed and the reports came back to the group.

What surprised us celibate priests and nuns in the group was that these married folk were being subjected to a lifestyle not unlike our own. We were amazed to hear the participants say that they had discovered a whole new range of delight and fulfilment in their relationships. They never realised what they had been missing.

My thoughts wandered to the many priests who belly-ache at the law of celibacy. They do not have the satisfaction of a physical marriage relationship, but what is there to stop them from enjoying the company of a good woman, a woman who might lead them as Beatrice led Dante, through the dark forest of their sexuality. We all need to be delivered from the over-stressed burden of the genital, to that many splendoured range of sexuality. We have all been made in the image and likeness of God, male and female.

Marriage is a definite area that is not mine to enter, but what is to rule out the kiss and the embrace of a good woman who might lead me on the same course as one who became a saint in company with another saint? I went to the library and opened the chapter entitled *Love that leads to union*, in *The Treatise on the Love of God* by St Francis de Sales. Commenting on the verse: *Let him kiss me with the kiss of his mouth,* in the Song of Songs, he writes: 'A kiss from all ages as by natural instinct, has been employed to represent love, that is union of hearts … The kiss at all times and among the most saintly men the world has had, has been a sign of love and affection. St Paul writing to the Romans and the Corinthians, says, 'Salute one another with a holy kiss.'

Celibacy may be a signpost to the kingdom of God, but it is no wooden sign that stands in lonely isolation, going nowhere itself.

'Never alone with a woman!'

Beloved,

You tell me that you inherited an uncomfortable and unsure understanding of your sexuality. You set yourself on a course that would build a security wall around your celibacy. Never alone with a man! Let me tell you that I got it the other way round and in sharply cut Latin, *Nunquam solus cum sola! Nunquam* means never. *Solus,* or *sola* in the feminine, means alone. *Fallen nature* was so constantly drummed into us, that we just did not trust ourselves.

When one is told that often enough, it engenders a sense of inadequacy and failure. I know one can easily go to the other extreme of presumption. But somewhere in between, there must be a happy mean. One is reminded of the words of the prophet Micah: 'This is what I ask of you, only this, to act justly, love tenderly and to walk humbly before your God.' (Micah 6:8)

Celibacy is a privileged place from which to act with justice and tenderness. But how can witness be given if it has never been lived out in the concrete? I'm thinking of the preacher who was told to overcome his timidity by looking out on his congregation and imagining they were all heads of green cabbage. He may have addressed them as *dearly beloved*, but did he treasure any of them as such? Tenderness and compassion and loyalty do not grow on trees or be found under heads of cabbage.

We celibate men could work with each other and pray with each other, but we were afraid to delight in each other's company and play together. The virtue of playfulness lies midway between being a complete bore on the one hand, and playing the buffoon on the other. Chaste loving, which is more akin to play than to work, might be seen as a happy mean between living in an iron mask on the one hand, and playing the harlot on the other.

Beloved, if we set our sights on living the safe life, keeping the rule and constitutions, we will get by sure enough. We'll not do much harm and we'll not do much good. We'll have our feet on the ground, but will hardly reach the stars. You and I may stand before the Judgement seat and say: 'Here I am Lord, with clean hands. See how I've never loved anyone.'

Beloved, let's have the courage to get out of our security boats and walk on the waters and learn to live and love before the face of Jesus, for his command is to love. We must of course discern this with faith, understanding and perception. Is it not reasonable that, if we are commanded to love, we must love somebody? And if it is love, it will ring true and bear fruit in due season.

There is a time for suffering, for trial, for going against the grain and our own personal inclination. But there is a time too, for loving with our inclination and attraction to the other. God expects us to be channels of his love, and instruments of healing for each other. This is especially true for those who are drawn by the Holy Spirit to love each other. Deep calls unto deep and heart cries to heart and the great sound that echoes through the hills and valleys of life is to love in a positive and dynamic manner. No need then to walk alone or without each other.

Delight in the Lord

Beloved,

There is a proverb about the dog that goes a bit of the road with everyone. He reminds me of those who flirt with life and with every one that takes their fancy. Loving is a serious business, especially the kind of love that is directed towards someone special.

I'm often asked where these wonderful special people are. Friendship is a gift and we have to wait with patient expectation until it comes. I want to share with you some lines from Psalm 36 which run:

Trust in the Lord and do good,
Then you will live in the land and be secure.
If you find your delight in the Lord,
He will grant your heart's desire.
Commit your life to the Lord.
Trust in him and he will act.
Be still before the Lord
And wait in patience.

I know a good mother who tells her children to pray earnestly, that they will meet the person God wants for them. I'm not saying that things will turn out exactly as they dream and desire. People may indeed get married and be happy. On the other hand, they may remain single, but not really alone. It is not God's wish for anyone to be an island standing out in the ocean. They may remain celibate, yet enjoy the companionship of another in a most delightful way.

Delighting in the Lord is the first step on the road to fulfilment. We first have to be on the receiving end of God's love. You know beloved, how we are enriched, as we rest in the presence of the Holy Eucharist. My own prayer at these sessions before the Blessed Sacrament exposed on the altar, is that we would become one living instrument of his healing love for all whom we meet.

Married persons must learn to seek the good of the other more than their own. Personal happiness is not something to run after as a prime objective. It is a by-product, a fall-out from wishing well to the beloved. As the prayer of St Francis has it, *It is in loving that we are loved*. Before wanting to be loved, seek after someone on whom you can pour out your love.

Before looking over the hedges at the green fields yonder, we must, as the Psalm says, first live in the land and be secure, where God has planted us. Blossom where you're planted. No need to envy the situation of another. Rest in and enjoy your own role in life. Enter into the here and now of your own existence. A rolling stone gathers no moss, and neither does it build bridges or mend fences.

Once when trying to make a decision, I remarked to my Spiritual Director that I would have to consult with a certain person to whom I had a commitment. At first he hesitated and said I should not have such a bond with another outside of commitment to the religious Order. When I told him that I did not see life in water-tight compartments of that kind, he smiled and said, 'Tell me more.'

My first step and indeed every step of the way, is to commit my life to the Lord, and not part of it, the whole of it. Like St Paul, I am learning to live and move in the Holy Spirit. This passage from his Letter to the Galatians is of prime importance for the one who wants to enter into the way of Christian love:

Learn to live and move in the Spirit. Then there is no danger of your giving way to the impulses of corrupt nature. The Spirit yields a harvest of love, joy, peace, patience, kindness, generosity.

My Body given for you

Beloved,

The celibate love of which I write to you is not a way out of the discipline of chastity to which we are all called. Neither is it a second class substitute for marriage. If anything, it is the high road to the heavenly marriage that exists between Christ, the Bridegroom, and his beloved spouse which is the church, and every individual member of the mystical Body that the church is. The love of which I write points to the true and deepest understanding of marriage. Perhaps it highlights something that is sometimes missed, yet is basic even to the norm of every marriage.

The Catholic Church has a theology and spirituality of marriage that is not always seen in its full splendour by contracting couples. Christian marriage is more than a contract, which is understood as an exchange of goods: *this gold and silver, I thee give, and with all my worldly goods I thee endow.* More deeply it is a covenant, which implies an exchange not merely of material things, but of minds and hearts, a union of persons. This personal covenant does not rest only on the horizontal place, but is meant to reflect something of the glory of the heavenly covenant.

The marriage covenant is an image of the covenant that God himself has made with his people. Even the Old Testament speaks of a marriage-bond or espousal, between Israel and the Lord. The promised land is seen as a marriage dowry and infidelity on the part of the people is spoken of in terms of adultery.

When I have the privilege of celebrating the Eucharist on the occasion of a wedding, I like to hone in on the words of the Consecration: 'This is my body which will be given up for you. This is the cup of my blood, the blood of the new and everlasting covenant. It will be shed for you and for all …'

This is the high point of the Wedding of the Lamb, as Divine love gives itself totally unto the shedding of blood. Christians who embrace the many-splendoured ambience of love, must turn to each other and say: 'This is my body, given up to and for you. For you would I gladly give my life's blood.'

Every Christian, single and married, is invited to this Wedding Feast of the Lamb, and not just as a guest, a best man or a bridesmaid. In the life of the Spirit, there are no spectators, no spinsters or bachelors. We are all spousally related to the Lord. Nuns at their profession like to consider themselves Brides of Christ. It would be a pity if this title were confined to professional religious.

It would be a pity too, if the relationship between Jesus and the individual soul remained simply on the vertical, and not carried over into the earthly bond between the lover and the beloved on the horizontal level of man and woman, whether married or celibate.

Jordan of Saxony expressed it to Diana: 'It is the Lord, who is the bond whereby we are bound together; in him my spirit is fast knit with your spirit. In him you are always without ceasing present to me, wherever I may wander.'

The Spirit informs the flesh

Beloved,

I am pondering over the words you sent me: 'Once the spirit informs the flesh, the flesh conforms to the spirit, and there is unity in the being and freedom to love. Reconciliation has taken place within. We are in the contented gaze of God, the Father, who thus sees the imprint of his Son in us.'

I know you did not do a course in scholastic philosophy, but seem to have been given this insight during your time before the Blessed Sacrament where you hold us both before the face of God. The word *inform* intrigues me, as it brings me back to my days of study at the feet of an eminent philosopher of the time. He assured us that he was not talking about information or informers, the mere passing on of knowledge. The scholastics, he told us, took this term from the ancient Greeks and *form* referred to 'that which gave being and character to any thing'.

I see that human sexuality is under the direction of God in its rhythms and functions. When we denigrate or refuse to allow his direction, confusion enters. You tell me that this direction is not a restriction so much as a benevolence and that there must be balance and integration in this God-given energy. When we are unsure, and fearful, it is because we are not fully aware of the underlying reality of God's love.

You tell me that it is not possible for you to communicate 'the nature and quality of divine love by word of mouth or through the intellect. The soul must have some experience of the mystical path and have been steadfastly guided to the point where it becomes a reality. The effects of this love may be explained but not the essence, since it must touch the soul experientially to be understood. However, if our meaning is love, we will grasp the nature of God's love. Its properties are manifold and deeply intimate, lending dynamism and direction, sureness of touch, precision and sophistication to the being. Once experienced, the soul can no longer be content with any other good.'

This is pretty high doctrine and it makes me feel so helpless and empty. I reckon that love like this is a gift from God and all I can do is leave myself open to it. Certainly I wish for it and desire it above anything else. I believe that Catherine of Siena was told by Jesus that the desire was all he asked for. I'm comforted by the very practical note on which you end. 'Divine love may have a lowly beginning, sparked off with someone whom God may send into your life. Like any discovery, this may take time and tension, but if you go with the river-flow of providence, you will find on the banks of the river, others with whom this love will intermingle and grow.'

Beloved, one person may be your unique friend, your focal point, your place of rest. From there, you reach out to others. Leaning on this one, you look outwards, as the babe nestling in its mother's arms looks sweetly and surely on the world around.

Wine, Women and Wealth

Beloved,

Be patient with me, as I bring you on a journey back in time. In 1953 as I was returning from studies in Rome, there was a message from the Master of the Order which said: 'This man is to be sent to Lourdes on his way back to Ireland in order to prepare himself for the preaching and promoting of the Rosary.' The journey which I made by public transport took me through the South-East of France.

About one hundred miles east of Lourdes I came across the fabulous walled city of Carcassonne, described as if it were one of the seven wonders of the world. I worked my way up the hill on which the old city is perched, and noted the massive touring buses, the long sleek motor cars, the pressing crowds of fashionable ladies and the cigar-puffing gentlemen. Mixed up with them were hundreds of young people in jeans with heavy packs on their backs. I was still wearing the white habit I had come in from Rome. It was no longer white, but it reminded me that once the founder of the Order of Preachers had wended his way through these same narrow streets which wind their way inside the great walls and towers of Carcassonne.

In one of the antique shops, I came across a small wooden sign, which caught my attention: It read:

> *Three things which rule and ruin a man:*
> *Wine, Women and Wealth!*

This, I learnt, was an expression of that terrible doctrine of the Albigensians, or to give them the name by which they are still known, the Catharists. These were extremists who claimed that only the spirit of a man came from God. Human flesh and all the physical creation, sun, moon, stars, animals etc. were the work of some evil principle.

Woman, the bearer of the human being, was held in particular abhorrence. This led on to a denial of the Incarnation, for they said, it was impossible that the Word of God, the Second Person of the Trinity could become flesh in a woman. To counteract this insidious teaching St Dominic came on the scene with the Hail Mary, which proclaimed: 'Blessed are you among women and blessed is the fruit of your womb.' According to pious legend, he heard a voice in the forest of Bouconne outside Toulouse telling him:

'Remember how the earth was dry and barren, until watered by the dew of the heavenly Ave. Go preach my Rosary and proclaim the mysteries of the Word made flesh and you will reap an abundant harvest.'

Thus could woman regain her dignity. In the light of the woman who bore the Son of God, human life would be esteemed, and transformed in the likeness of Jesus.

Beloved, the Hail Mary is addressed not only to the Lady, Mary of Nazareth, but it is spoken to each and every one of us. The Lord's wish is that every soul should bring forth the Christ child. Know, beloved, that I often speak these words in prayer to your dear self and entreat the Lord to make you full of grace to the measure of his great giving, so that you too bring forth Jesus in your life.

This has been well stated in the poem by Sr Agnes Vollman:

> The Virgin longed to see the face
> Of Him she bore.
> She full of grace
> Must wait nine months to gaze upon
> Her God, her Christ, her Son.
>
> At last, O ever-mounting joy,
> He's born, her boy.
> And lo, his sacred features
> Are like one other creature's.
>
> His lips, his eyes, his brow,
> Formed in her till now,
> Are but her own, Hers, alone.

The longing, is it stilled?
Ah no, for God hath willed,
Unto eternity
Her task should be:
To mould his features,
Once again,
This time, within all men.

I have often altered the last line of the poem, to read: *this time within all creatures*. Mary is Queen of all creation and the glory of this mystery of the Incarnation, this Mother and Child scheme of salvation, embraces the entire realm of creation. The Holy brooding Spirit that came upon Mary at Nazareth, longs to over-shadow the whole waiting world.

Start with Someone

Beloved,

As a priest, I have to reach out to many who are studying for long years at college. They want to live life to the full. They have energy to burn and love to share. This goes across the whole range of living, and their sexuality is one of their priorities.They may not expect much from a dried up prune such as they suspect I am. Truth is that if they are right, I'm just irrelevant.

That's why I want to declare my situation. For many years I was indeed a dried up workaholic. I was frightened to stop in case I might have to admit that what I did was more important than what I was. Workaholics are more interested in themselves and their accomplishments than in the lives of others. The workaholic is self-centred and more concerned with personal survival than the happiness of the other. Trouble is, there very often is no significant other.

I was once invited to join a Marriage Encounter Weekend. I went along and saw married couples arrive in a matter-of-fact manner, only to go home at the end of the sessions, as exuberantly joyful pairs. I went off, the same as I'd arrived. They said that for me, the parish or the community was to be my partner. Fifteen wives or a whole parish of fifteen thousand! You must be joking. I was plunged back into my working duds again. I did try loving the whole bunch, sometimes together and sometimes one after the other. It proved a polygamous disaster.

A very wise woman remarked that this kind of loving was a cop-out, a recipe for loving no one and nothing. 'Start with one,' she said. 'From the stability and certainty of that love, you can reach out to others. Love without expression is sterile. But make sure that it is love you are seeking, learn to live and move in the Spirit. Watch for God's timing and do not awake love before its time. Never forget that love, as St Paul put it, is patient.'

Love is kind; love is not envious or boastful or arrogant or rude. It does not insist on its own way; it is not irritable or resentful; it does not rejoice in wrong-doing, but rejoices in the truth. It bears all things, believes all things, hopes all things, endures all things. (1 Cor 13).

If only we can take our minds off our own needs and reach out to the needs of the other, the imperious drive of genitality can be steered into the ways of the spirit. Many are frigid and they call it chastity, thus giving weight to misconceptions and half truths and off-centred views. A call to chastity is of necessity a call to true love.

Christ came to teach us how to love. For this he was crucified. Those who seek his inspiration cannot expect to do so without similarly stretching out hands and opening hearts to sacrifice. The question I must ask as I set out on the road to love, is this: Is there anyone in this world, who is more precious to me than my own existence?

Is there anyone for whom I would gladly lay down my life?

Be Vigilant

Beloved,

'Be calm, but vigilant because your enemy the devil is prowling round, like a roaring lion, looking for someone to eat. Stand up to him strong in faith' says St Peter.

At Night Prayer we add the words: 'Into your hands, I commend my spirit.' We need the twin guardians of watchfulness and prayer, as we walk through the forest of the divine mystery of love.

There is life and growth in the forest, but it is a dark place, beloved, where danger may lurk. It takes courage to live in love. To change the image, we have to respect power lines of electric current. We put up a notice: *Keep away*, yet know that without this power we are without light and heat. Lines of life are lines of danger, but only when handled carelessly.

Satan tries to tangle up our life-lines. On the one hand he gets us to ignore and despise material things, and on the other hand to over-indulge or abuse the things of earth and in particular the gift of our sexuality. We must be aware that there are alien forces that work against the Divine plan for us.

This is where we need to cling to Jesus, the Divine Humanity, the Reconciler of the warring elements that rise up in human nature. Only Divine love can change the distorted area in the being. It is of the essence of God to change what is twisted and troubled, and it is through Christ that this comes about.

Emotions and feelings and mere wishing, these are not enough. We are, however, equipped with one faculty that can open the way to this coming of Christ. It is the human will. Love is a decision of the will, not an urge of the flesh. Such urges and instincts can fail and lead astray. They may be good servants, but they are poor masters. The will, one with the Lord Jesus, must be in control.

When Jesus becomes Lord in our lives, and our hearts are one with his Sacred Heart, there will be freedom in loving, children will be protected against violation, parents will be honoured and peace will flow out from families.

Jesus calls us to live out the implications of the Word made flesh dwelling among us. With our lives built around the dynamic presence of Our Lord in the Eucharist, and reaching out to touch him in the mysteries of the Rosary, we can experience the power that goes out from the Divine Humanity of Jesus.

Jesus, the Reconciler and Healer takes over the land of our being, and the warring factions within are set at rest. The divided land of flesh and spirit becomes the land of promise and we are made whole. (Cf 2 Chronicles: 7:14)

As we claim the land of our own being for Christ, the enemies from within and without are defeated and you and I, beloved, become kings and queens and are given power to bring healing, peace and great love to others.

PS

The possibility of walking celibately in love is grounded in the knowledge that our own humanity shares somehow in the divine humanity of Jesus and that in consequence we are a divinised humanity, no longer slaves of fallen nature.

You might like to know that some theologians have had difficulty with this expression *The Divine Humanity*. However, the term is to be found in several Christian writings and has been fully developed in the published works of Vladimir Soloviev, the spiritual father of Russian Catholicism, styled the Newman of Russia. Other references can be seen in *Catholicism* by Henri de Lubac and in *The Office of Peter and the Structure of the Church* by Hans Urs Von Balthasar. In one of the last works of the beloved Pope John Paul II, *Memory and Identity: Personal Reflections*, we find this statement: 'The Second Vatican Council bases its teaching on the great wealth of earlier doctrinal reflection upon Christ's divine humanity.'

Pray and Play

Beloved,

You taught me a lesson when I called on you last week and I have been turning it over in my mind ever since. I'm not sure if I've come to terms with it yet. One of the significant factors in our relationship is that it has to be a learning experience for both of us.That is a humbling fact, which reminds me of what the Master told us: 'Learn of me because I am meek and humble of heart.'

You know how attached I am to the Rosary and how I never venture out without being sure it's snuggled safely in my pocket. Anyway, when you were speaking to John and myself, I let the two of you talk on your own. I took the opportunity to slip into freewheel, with eyes half-shut and the beads in my fingers. I was lazily pondering the new mystery of the Transfiguration and marvelling to myself at the same time about the transfigured glory which our love reflects.

Suddenly you remarked: 'When you pray, pray, but when you come to see me, keep your eyes on me. Do you think Jesus would have been fingering his beads while he was engaged with the woman at the well of Samaria? There is a time and place for everything.'

You sure surprised me, beloved, and I have to work on that one. The only thing I can say right now is that you remind me of how St Catherine of Siena treated her good friend Raymund of Capua. She scolded him for nodding off to sleep while she was pouring out her soul in profound spiritual wisdom.

Women never seem to understand how sleepy we poor men can get when we get away from the world of business and serious game-play. A certain major religious superior once said, 'I'm sick and tired of alcoholics and workaholics. They all need to have a good woman to look after them and bring them into the truth.'

Something along the same lines happened to me one day

when my niece, Anne, came to the house. Her mother left her in my care while she went shopping. I was trying to get through a serious book, in preparation for a sermon next day. I had switched off the child on the floor and the game of Leggo that was so intriguing to her. Out of the silence, a voice came: 'Put down your book. This is playtime. I can't play on my own, I need you, down here on the carpet with me.'

What could I do but put my book, my pen and paper aside and get on the floor, on my knees in fact. Shakespeare has something about 'sermons in stones and books in the running brooks.' All I can say is that the next day's sermon wrote itself, but it was far from the book in my hand. It was from my heart and it is still unfinished business.

St Benedict has a motto for his monks, *Ora et Labora*, Pray and labour. I'll have to add, but make time for play!

Aelred on Spiritual Friendship

Beloved,

Thanks for letting me have your copy of *Spiritual Friendship*, the classic by Aelred of Rievaulx. I was intrigued by the fact that he goes right back to Cicero and quotes so much from his work, *De Amicitia*. I was particularly taken by the words: 'I call them more beasts than men, who say that they should take no pleasure in the good of another or seek to love or be loved.'

The only problem I have with Aelred's notion of friendship is that it seems to have no place for women. It is constrained to the monastic setting and deals only with friendship between the brethren. I don't know, beloved, how he would have dealt with a relationship such as ours. The Cistercian lifestyle in any event was an all-male situation within the enclosure walls. Incidentally I'm not terribly impressed by the title of Aelred's Book, *Spiritual Friendship*. I would just say *friendship* without any adjective. We are not pure spirits, but creatures of flesh and blood and spirit, who live and love with the totality of our being.

The early Friars like the Dominicans and Franciscans did not have vows of stability, ensuring that they live in any enclosed space. They were itinerants, and women played a significant role in their apostolic lives. Some more conservative characters at the time feared for these young strolling friars, but St Dominic took his courage in hand and sent them out under the protection of the Blessed Virgin Mary, to deal with the Puritan Catharists of the day.

You fill up my Senses

Beloved,

I grew up with Frank Duff, that giant of a man who was the founder of the Legion of Mary. While he strode the world like a colossus, he was one of the meekest of men. Reminds me of Moses of whom it was said that while meek and gentle, when he stood up to speak, his words became a flaming torch. Frank presided over world-shaking spiritual events, surrounded by serious minded colleagues, but every now and then, he would bring his mother to the theatre, or would take himself off on his sturdy bicycle to enjoy the pleasant Irish countryside.

When I was younger, I took myself and life very seriously. I can't say that I took much time to stop and stare and taste the loveliness of creation. Needless to say, I never found time to love, or experienced much need to be loved. My mind was always in overdrive and my senses were allowed to drag along as a kind of baggage. My father brought me to football games, but I was never able to share his exhilaration or to live over the thrills and spills of the match. He must have been saddened, but I never knew or cared. I was locked in my intellectual cocoon.

Then one day, beloved, you played for me your recording of James Galway on his silver flute. *You fill up my senses … like a dream in the night.* That started off my discovery of the senses, to learn for myself what the philosophers had been telling me: The senses are the gateways to the mind. 'There is nothing in the mind, that was not first in the senses.'

There is a time for voiding the senses, for purifying them and even denying them. But that is not the end of the journey. As God enters through the spirit, he enters also into the body. But until we have joined him willingly where he is, in our land, there is pain. What he promised, the joy that no one can take from us, is at the end of that journey. When the soul has grasped this, it will never falter until it reaches that point where true freedom is, and all its expressions. The soul knowing that it now has all these freedoms and is in God, cannot be deprived of this inexpressible joy.

Unified in God, the whole being comes alive. It views everything afresh, as for the first time. We are unified and prepared to enter the kingdom of God from which nothing is missing, even in this world. Some celibates do not understand that they are called to the enjoyment of deep love. They are meant to enjoy love, but with the understanding that there is no enjoyment outside God.

The love that we seek is one that never dies. If the ground of our being is still the ground of unwatered nature, then death will come and take our love away. 'A man will reap what he sows. If nature is his seed-ground, nature will give him a perishable harvest. If his seed-ground is the spirit, it will give him a harvest of eternal life.' (Gal: 6:8)

Let us pray, beloved, that the Spirit of the living God may fall gently upon us, *as dew in April that falleth on the grass*. With the warring elements of our being reconciled through Jesus, the Reconciler, peace will pervade the land of our being.

Claude who nearly blew up!

Beloved,

In case you may be wondering where all the others who may have an experience like ours are hiding, I want to tell you about Claude. I came across him in a letter he received on 19 July 1932. It was reprinted in an English Catholic magazine. The author was telling him to go away into the woods and read St Aelred's treatise on *Spiritual Friendship*. He goes on to tell Claude that his temptation has been always towards Puritanism, a narrowness, a certain inhumanity.

Beloved, I have copied this out from the magazine, and am sending it, as it is a confirmation of our own thought.

Dear Claude,

Your tendency was almost towards the denial of the hallowing of matter. You were in love with our Lord but not properly with the Incarnation. You were really afraid. You thought that if you once relaxed, you'd blow up. You bristled with inhibitions. They nearly killed you. They nearly killed your humanity. You were afraid of life because you wanted to be a saint ...

The artist in you saw beauty everywhere. The would-be saint in you said, 'That's frightfully dangerous.' The novice in you said, 'Keep your eyes tight shut.' The Claude in you nearly blew up. If P hadn't come into your life, you might have blown up. I believe P will save your life. I shall say a Mass in thanksgiving for what P has been, and done, to you. You have needed P a long time. Aunts are no outlet. Nor are stout and elderly provincials.

Don't you see that you have got a talent for friendship, and that it is very dangerous, and that nevertheless it is worse than dangerous to wrap it in a napkin and that it has got to be used? Don't imagine P will be the last one you'll fall in love with. You were meant to love P and to be of service to P. You will find that God will use you for others too ....

Your only chance is to go on loving P. If you stopped, you'd miss God. If you thought the only thing to do was to retire into your shell you'd never see how lovely God was. You must love P and look for God in P. Keep reminding yourself that God is in P and that God is in you: that you're both monstrances of God.

Whoever P was, I fancy Claude and herself must by now be roaming the forests of heaven together. I like the expression *monstrances of God*. Perhaps they would have sat together before the monstrance of the Blessed Sacrament and experienced something of the radiance of divine love which pours out from the heart of Jesus in the Blessed Eucharist. You and I know what peace and healing fills our whole beings as we do our time of adoration. If Jesus were not in our loving, it would be a poor thing, withering even as it flowered. We must not waste our love. We want it to blossom like the rose and turn the desert into a place of springs. So let's not just look at each other, but face the rising sun of the face of Jesus in his secret place.

Where Love is, there is God

Beloved,

Love is the great Christian experience. It brings sweetness and strength. It flows and leads you true. We must not think that as long as we can control love or dampen it down we can play safe. That is unworthy of such a gift. The reason we refuse love, is that we are often frightened of the demands it can make. We may not be ready for the responsibilities it brings. Real love brings pain and suffering. We have to give up much for the sake of the king- dom. One has to go beneath the surface and stop flirting with it. Once you have tasted it, you run after it. And you find it brings its own control, its own momentum.

This control has to be learnt by personal checks and balances, and by giving up on mere personal satisfaction. It can't always be gleaned from the experience of others. If you are loving and not becoming an individual, beware. Real love carries with it its own good reason. If your security in loving consists in giving so much provided you get so much, you are on the wrong road. You've got to go alone and find God on your own first. Only then, can you love another. There must be no pretence or deceit in loving.

Love is a mysterious phenomenon which has to be experi- enced to be understood. But those who have loved and have the capacity to love, know that love is indivisible. If it is really love, you can't compartmentalise it. You experience it in your being; in its purity love will lead you true. Love has only one source, and only one end and one existence.

Satan wants you to think that love is some mischievous thing that God doesn't really approve of. He doesn't want you to ask where does it come from, how is it? He wants to disturb you into thinking that if you steal it, it will be the real thing, but if it comes from God, it will be defective. And this is just not true.

If you follow the initial disciplines of love, so as to create in yourself the capacity to love, love when it comes will bring God.

When love has come, God has come. Where charity and love are, there is God.

Beloved, don't be tempted to think of charity as a cheap hand-out. It is a matter of giving first place to God, abandoning ourselves to the overwhelming tide of his jealous love. If we do not give him that standing, we are on a road to nowhere. We must not idolise our friends or relations or our superiors. We may have to renounce our possessions. We may have to travel in darkness and in the shadow of death. Yet in the midst of all that, beloved, let us walk before the face of God and his face will shine upon us and light up the way.

In Love forever!

Beloved,

If God said through Gabriel to Mary, 'Rejoice ...', what else was she supposed to do but be joyful? The notion that the body has to die and go into the ground before it is dead, is nonsense. God came that you might have life and have it abundantly. We all know we'll have abundant life in heaven, so it must mean, that the abundance will start now. In fact, the being gives up only the road to darkness, despair, despondency and walks in the light. God wants to teach love, not some emasculated kind of loving, or the love of some eunuch, but a share in his own love.

Sometimes when people fall in love, they are not free in their loving. There can be areas of darkness, and the basis for a solid happiness may be lacking. When things go wrong, they say that being in love is a springtime or summer affair. It's not made for the mellow fruitfulness of autumn or the snows of winter.

But why should the beautiful die? Why with a heart that is ever faithful and a will that makes a daily decision to love, should the fragrance of the summer rose fade and die beneath the winter snows? For those who have found the fire of divine love, the golden rose of being in love will burst into a forest flame at the sight and sound of the beloved.

God is the beginning, the source and end of love. The will of God is not primarily some horizontal path. There is that, but the will of God is the alignment of the human being with the world-stirring mystery of Christ, yesterday, today, the same forever. In his burning heart, we live and move and have our being. In him there is no shadow or alteration of love. The establishment of Christ in the being takes human co-operation.

The true celibate, who groans at times as he struggles with his celibacy, still knows in his heart, that this is the high road, if he can take it. He or she is the one who is truly free to love. We have to be alone and look into the face of Christ, to grasp what this path means, and in loneliness we have to make answer.

Beloved, you are always reminding me of St Augustine saying, *Love and do as you will*. Inherent in that statement is the imperious and willing drive to God. Everything else is secondary to this relentless seeking, this pushing on to God, as grace draws. Draw us, Lord, and let us run after you on this highway of love.

Beloved, let's not forget that it takes three to love, you and me and God, who in himself is a Holy Trinity.

The Mountain of Love

Beloved,

In case you are becoming fearful of this high-hill road to the mountain of love, let me assure you that we are simply attuning our step to the rhythm of quiet abandonment to Divine providence. When you were going into hospital, and were nervous about what was to happen, I gave you this simple remedy that I have always found helpful myself. It is to pray with Jesus on the Cross: 'Father, into your hands, I commend my spirit.' Even when the dentist's drill seems to be coming near a sensitive area, I let the words whisper themselves into my ear. When they were putting me asleep for the operation, I just looked at the lovely hands of the surgeon and the nurses and saw them as the outstretched hands of the Father in heaven and prayed quietly, 'Into your hands, Lord.'

Abandonment to God's action spills over on the body and even on the nerves and muscles. It touches the very sinews of life. It lets you float gently on a sea of tranquillity. When you are abandoned, you take a measured view of everything in life. You become more shriven and acute in worldly matters, when you are thus detached. Your emotions will not get mixed up to let you make mistakes. You can let the follies and the foibles of others pass. What we sometimes see as obstacles in our path may well be signposts, which in our rush we either knock down or ignore. The abandoned soul will not rush on impetuously, nor on the other hand will it lie down on the road as if it had reached a dead-end. The gallant abandoned person keeps marching on until stopped, and when stopped is grateful, as when a man climbing a mountain is stopped and told to take another route to avoid danger ahead.

We may groan and grumble at how things seem to be working out. We say, how can there be a just God? Believe me, beloved, I'm glad I don't always get the justice I think I deserve. If I got what I deserve, I might be unpleasantly surprised.

Abandonment has taught me to pray: 'Lord, I don't look for justice. I'll settle for your mercy.'

Beloved, it was yourself who said: 'Don't worry about what you achieve or don't achieve. God can accomplish in one second of grace, all that you might have striven for in a lifetime. Often we spoil what God is going to give us, by grasping and trying to possess in advance what he is going to give sweetly in his own time. What God is doing at the essence of your being is more important than what is going on at the edges.'

This is not to say that we should impose a superhuman level on the ways of nature. Life with all its demands has to be lived, but always with an inner eye that must be kept clear for the signs of the love that are leading us steadily onwards and upwards.

Abandonment to the rhythm of God

Beloved,

Abandonment is a direct way to God. It is a walk in faith and it becomes stronger by use. Intimacy with God is only truthfully understood in abandonment. We do not climb from one plateau to another to find God's will. Abandonment is like two clouds weaving together, one pressing into the other yielding and enfolding. So our wills are attuned to God's rhythms and movements. Peace is the barometer that will lead you true. 'And your ears shall hear a word behind you, saying: This is the way, Walk in it.' (Isaiah 30:20)

The rhythm of God is beating through all humanity and all must be given up to God. In his time he is going to sweep into you and right through you. This will in no way rob you of your humanity, but simply transform it, so that it shares in his divinity. This is the result of the life, death and glory of Jesus. If you let that Passover rhythm beat out to the last, it will end in a symphony.

In this way of experiential love, the way is straight, but the terrain is broad. In the journey to the inner land, you will find your personal dignity, your true self. You must not, however, see yourself as locked in to this inner space, opening a window now and then to see how things are on the outside. We do not live with one eye shut to reality. We have to live in both worlds at once. The rivers of the inner land overflow their banks and flow into the desert to blossom like the rose.

Thanks, beloved, for your poem which so splendidly says it all:

> Love is the tide that returns,
> running full and free with God,
> to flow out into our days
> taking us through the rich park lands of Summer,
> the desolate forlorn terrain of Winter
> and the pleasant surprises of Spring and Autumn.

> It is the dream, we dream along with God,
> as locked in the eternal rhythm,
> for which all has well been lost and won,
> we enter Paradise at last.

Prayer takes us to the paradise of divine love. It touches the borders of infinity and reaches to the depths of the inner being. It attunes us to the Divine will, and makes it sweet to linger in love with the Lord. Prayer is the dream we dream along with God, as locked in the eternal rhythm, we move surely into love, the love for which all else has been lost, as we enter paradise, even on earth.

Don't worry beloved, about your ability to perform great works. Performance is peripheral. God reads the inner heart. Had he meant to judge you by performance, he might as well have made you an actor. You may suffer, but the sword that pierces the heart is carving out the personal space where you may flourish. Sorrow builds a bridge into the infinite and becomes the meeting-place of God with the soul.

Your land may be ploughed with deep furrows that show on your hands and face, but in your soul, beloved, the heavenly Ploughman has buried seeds that will reap a harvest. We may sow in sorrow, but with the love of God binding us together and beckoning us on, we will come home full of joy, carrying our sheaves.

In little ways

Beloved,

I thank you for the poem you wrote for me when I was going away. Its fragrance will keep me going on my journeys. You mention the little things I did for you. Rest assured nothing is a chore when done for one who is another self. Where there is love, there is no labour. While the poem is clearly written in haste on a scrap of paper, I want to set it out here, so that others may learn from it:

> When you are gone my little one
> Whatever shall I do,
> To talk or dance in words
> At night or in the twilight through.
> And who will understand me then
> Or do the littlest things,
> To bring my heart to greater heights
> And lead me to the King.

Love has indeed to do the littlest things as well as attempt the greatest. Love must prove itself in deeds, not just the Sunday summery day things, but the works of Monday and winter night things. It is easy to be a cat licking the cream off the milk and leaving the skimmed remains for others to drink.

Ann Morrow Lindbergh, the American poet and essayist who wrote a long essay that questions the meaning of existence for the individual woman, has something similar to say. Ann was the wife of Charles Augustus Lindbergh, the aviator who made the first solo flight across the Atlantic Ocean in the famed plane, *Spirit of St Louis*. They often flew together when he pioneered new routes to Latin America, Asia and Europe. She was not only a devoted wife, but she was ever ready to do the little things and the steadfast splendid things that cemented their union.

That is evident in the lines she wrote in *Locked Rooms and*

Open Doors: 'People talk about love as though it was something you could give like an armful of flowers. And a lot of people give love like that, just dump it down on top of you, a useless, strong-scented burden ... Love is the force in you, that enables you to give other things. It is the motivating power. It enables you to give strength and power and freedom and peace to another person ...'

When we first met, beloved, I was a pretty self-centred person. It is one of the occupational hazards of celibate priests. We are so much on our own and don't have children to care for or take us out of our smugness. It is so easy for us to look for creature comforts in food and drink and golf and holidays, with only ourselves in mind. When not centred on the Lord, it is easy to fall into a bachelor mentality.

I loved my brethren in community, but I confess that I never cried when one of them went away or even when someone in the house died. I just moved up one place in the refectory and got on with dinner. I must not speak for the others. They may have been walking another path of which I was ignorant.

All I know, beloved, is that you came my way and walked alongside me in my blindness. I took your hand and you led me in paths I knew not.

Virgin Bride

Beloved,

Joan has written to say that she is about to take a vow of chastity and wants to live as a virgin. She has no intention of becoming a nun, but wants to witness to the kingdom of God living an ordinary life in the world. She is praying to Jesus in these words: 'In your mercy you arrange it that I have only you to love. To be truly your bride, completely given over to your interests, the heart and the soul must be truly virginal, having no affection, no attachment except to yourself.'

I would have thought along those same lines at a certain stage in my own religious journey. We were more or less trained in that fashion. *None but thyself, O Lord!*

Can this be right? Only you Lord to love, no affection except yourself. Have we to put on a clinical cold face to our neighbour? It reminds me of the engraving on the Yeats gravestone: *Cast a cold eye on life on death. Horseman pass by.*

Beloved, how would you feel if I told you that I had given up my affection for you, because I was called to love only Jesus? I doubt if Jesus himself would approve. I propose writing back to Joan, and while I don't want to disturb or dampen down her ardour, I would prefer to word her prayer like this: 'Dear Jesus, I love you with all my mind, my heart and soul. I want to have no affection that is not rooted in you. From henceforth, I give myself, all that I am and all that I have, to your loving care. Help me to find you in every one I meet, to entrust to your Sacred Heart all those whom I love and care for.'

Since in Christ we live and move and have our being and know that in him all things hold together, how can there be anything or anyone that is outside the range of his arms? When we arrive at the stage that we see only Jesus, it can only be because we have brought everything and everyone under his Lordship, and are living in the covenant which has been established in his blood. Then there is no division or dichotomy between the sacred and the secular. Life is no longer lived in watertight compartments of flesh and spirit. We are whole and wholesomely holy.

Every Christian, whether married or celibate, is invited to be sealed by this blood covenant, in the all-embracing marriage of the Lamb and his bride, the church. And as Jesus has given us an example, we are meant to live in this covenant with each other. I suppose there is a special sense in which we speak of Sr X becoming a bride of Christ on her profession day. But the plain Christian fact is that we are all called to be brides of Christ and are invited to the marriage-feast, not just when we enter heaven, but right here and now.

I'm thinking of the many men and women who have lived in steadfast loyalty to each other and to the sacred vows they took before the altar. I think of my own married sister, and of the dedication of her life to husband and children. She lives in a constant state of prayer and union with the Lord. Jesus is King of her life and Mary is Queen and they are first in her life and affections. If she is not a bride of Christ, what is she?

The basic attraction of all creatures is towards the Creator, who is at once the summit and the source of all love. Lesser loves are sanctioned and supported by the divine love. Outside this dynamic, they are all simply rushing towards the cliffs of death, like the Gadarine swine. That is why every soul cries out: *Draw me and we will run after thee.* In saying this we desire that all whom we love will run after him in this blessed race to the new creation. Outside of this drawing, life just withers and dies in a winter wasteland. But when we have yielded our wills to this drawing, the bodily faculties follow in train and all the whole being, body, soul and spirit, sing in tune, *We will run after thee.*

In his work, *Between Community and Society*, Fr Thomas Gilby has written: 'Charity is alien to nothing human, because it is the form, exemplar and end of all loves. It is not a high thin jet, but a flood. It flows into every interest and into objects not in themselves sacred.'

The Song of Songs is for everyone to sing. I sing it to you now, beloved:

Arise, my love, my fair one and come away.
For now Winter is past ...
O my dove ...
Let me see your face
Let me hear your voice, for your voice is sweet
and your face is lovely.

I write to you beloved, not to belittle the splendour of formal re-ligious life, but simply to lighten the overload that sometimes is carried by those who take vows of celibacy. Married or single, lay or religious, we all travel in the same strong sweet boat of love. Let's not be surprised if like Peter, we have to leave our boats to walk on waters that will bring us to ever new and exciting horizons.

There is only one love

Beloved,

I have already told you that I never keep our relationship a secret. It is not enough to sit with you alone. I want to walk with you before the world, as I love you before the face of the one who is Lord of us all. So when I told one of my priest colleagues about our relationship, he smiled and said, 'Gabriel, it is your age! I'm young and full of sexual energy and couldn't cope with a love like yours.'

Scripture says that there is a time for everything, a time to plant and a time to dig up, a time to love and a time to hate. I can't speak for others but now that I am old and grey, and in love, I know that I often feel like twenty, and that when I was seventeen, I often felt like seventy!

When I was a youthful clerical student walking to the Pro-Cathedral with lots of other black-robed students, the teenagers on the side walks were singing: *Love makes the world go round.* 'Stop that song,' one of them whispered, 'the priesteens wouldn't understand.'

Perhaps we didn't, which is more the pity. We were trained intellectually and our heads were filled with chunks of philosophy and theology. At the other end of the scale, we had a spiritual director who gave us splendid lectures and personal direction which lifted us into a world above and beyond. But neither of the two disciplines seemed to merge.

As for physical formation, football and long walks were high on the college agenda. Strenuous exercise was supposed to tire us out and burn out feelings or emotions which might be presumed to turn our hearts in the soft ways of love. We were being trained to manly toughness, and being initiated into a sphere which moved on a different orbit to that of those we thought of as *living in the world*.

Heads and hands, faces and feet were all tuned and trained to state of the art standards, but much of what lay in between slumbered like Vesuvius. For some, the volcano may never have awakened. For many, it began to rumble and rebel only in much later years.

Our teachers told us of the divisions and distinctions of love, but they served it up to us on blocks of ice. We heard of charity or divine love. We knew of the earthy loves we might call natural or just plain human. We had been brought up with the instinctive love for parents and brothers and sisters. We knew something too of the love of friendship and the love of country. Added to all these was the eros love of man and woman, which we had noted to some degree between our parents or among the young couples of our time.

But the sad part about our understanding was that we saw these loves not as simply distinguished from each other but as divided and existing in separate water-tight compartments. A study of *The Four Loves* by the highly esteemed C. S. Lewis, for me, at least, only added to the confusion. It seemed to me as if love had been well and truly quartered.

Lewis had dealt with the four classical divisions of love, with particular emphasis on the friendship of the common room of the professors and the classroom of the scholars. Only on the last page was the question of divine love, *agape* love of the new Testament, brought up. Lewis was humble enough to say that here he is out of his depth and leaves the matter for others more competent in this field.

The trouble with such treatment is that one is confirmed in the thinking that natural love and divine love are two poles that never meet. I believe that this kind of polarisation is the cause of much schizophrenic living in the whole area of human sexuality, for both married and celibate people.

The truth of the matter is that there is but one love. God is Love, spelt indeed with a capital L. Without divine love all creature-loves are deprived of sustenance, for the simple reason that in God alone do we live and move and have our being. Without this central core of love, no other love can be.

It is not a question of adding on a layer of divine love, as it were, to top up our natural reserve. In the concrete situation there just isn't any reserve tank or starting up supply of natural love. All is fuelled and fired by the divine spark from beginning to the end.

This interplay of human and divine love is sensitively touched on, by a certain mystic of our time:

> O Love, be not obscured by love,
> O Love, heal the wounds
> That love receives,
> As it seeks to be,
> So that love might
> Love become thy gift to me.

Divine love in no way takes from the delight and the intensity of human love. Rather does it enhance it. Jesus does not wish to rob us of this earth's true joy. He came to bring life and that we might have it more abundantly. But this abundance is short-circuited and often missed by the mistake of seeking first the earthly love of this kingdom.

One notes a great deal of writing on the subject of love and loving, which begins on the earth and never seems to get off the ground. Even in the delicate area of loving, for celibates, a great deal of writing and talking centres on human need and creature-comfort. It tends to be ego-centric, asking, 'How and where, can I find someone to love me?' It might be more helpful to ask, 'Who is there for me to reach out to in love?'

I was a Workaholic

Beloved,

A certain religious Superior was heard to say, concerning some members of his community: 'I'm sick and tired of alcoholics and workaholics. I wish they could find a good someone to look after them. They're fundamentally lonely and need a good woman to love them. Rules and sanctions are no substitute for love.'

I can readily identify with that. For many years I was busy about many things. I found success and satisfaction in work and achievement. I was a goal-setter, and an achiever and there are records and documents to prove it. There may well be ten thousand names and addresses in those records. But they are only paper records and fading files that bring neither life nor love. I knew all about these people on these records. They are clients and consumers, workers and co-workers. But where does that leave me? Where does it lead? To a lonely self-centred old age with nothing to hand on but these paper pages and documents.

Knowing about you and how to handle your affairs and make them mine was a poor substitute for knowing you and loving you. But that's where I got stuck. I was not an alcoholic, but I sure was a workaholic. I was surrounded by projects and even by people, yet I was alone. The projects were on my desk and I could wade through them in time. The people could be counted and checked and dealt with. But I can't say that I cared about or loved any of them. Enough, they had paid their subscription and remained in their files.

Love knows no labour, for all is sweet to the lover. May we be preserved from the army of loveless celibates. Not only do they carry lead in their shoes and iron in their hearts. They go on to lay intolerable burdens on others. And I was one of that army of the lonely and loveless.

Then beloved, you came on the scene. Suddenly, programmes and projects were no longer enough. There was something missing. There was no centre to my life, no one to make things live, no love to make things matter. True, the word of God was my spiritual centre, but I needed to find a word made flesh with hands to hold me and a heart to love me. Even Jesus of 2000 years ago was not enough. I needed to meet him in flesh and blood. I needed not only the Eucharist, but a eucharistic partner with whom I could find communion.

As if the heavens had opened I felt a strong wind blow through the structures and the strictures of my being. I wanted to live no longer in a world where the computer dictated the pace and rhythm of life. I needed to break out of my cocoon of selfishness and artificial illusion of success. In a word, I needed to love, not just to be loved but to open my heart, to fling wide my arms, to reach out and hold someone in love.

I reach out to you, beloved, because I need love, not just at the receiving end, but most of all at the point of giving. I need to look at you, to listen to you, to touch you, to worship at the shrine that you are. You have become the tabernacle wherein to find life and love, rest and restoration. You are my eucharistic partner and we share the one table of the King.

Until I met you

Beloved,

I never loved until I met you. I was a man of books and lectures, one who dabbled in theories and philosophies. My motto was truth, and I thought it was enough to keep within the rails of logic and reason. I did not know that life is larger than logic. I did not realise that love could set things on fire and that it sometimes burned up the leaves of paper logic.

I beavered away like a mole in the dark. I thought that I would get by on judgement-day, by the record of my works and the sheer amount of my prayers. In the back of my mind, I kept the words: 'In the evening of life, we will all be judged on love.' But they seemed vague and outside the range, where I felt secure, going round and round. Doing the rounds is an occupational hazard for ministers of religion. Evening was a long time off and I wanted to labour as if it were to be always noontide.

I stopped now and then, but only to pass judgement on others, superficial judgement at that. I dared not stop to look with love, or listen with concern, to those who walked and worked beside me. I dared not stop lest they question or discover me. Undiscovered I was lost, lost to myself, lost to those who may have been searching for me, lost to the God who must have been looking out for me.

I could not linger to love. I thought it sinful to do so. How could I be found wasting my time, the time of others and indeed God's time? God's time did not come into the reckoning. When evening came, I would set my clock to new time, but for now I lived by my own old time. I had as yet not discovered the secret of the one who wrote:

> When the time of our particular sunset comes,
> our accomplishments won't matter a great deal,
> but the clarity and care
> with which we have loved others
> will speak with vitality of the gift of life
> we have been for each other.

Then one sunset, beloved, you appeared and walked with me with sureness of step and with grace-filled timing. You came in the splendour of a light that bore down on my mole-like existence.

I was blinded by the sunshine that shone from your face and poured out of your soul. 'Linger in love with me,' you said. Your words were a prayer and they led me to linger in love with the Lord.

You were my Zephaniah and you let the Lord renew me in his love and exult over me with loud singing. You were my Daughter of Zion, and with you, I began to sing and dance for joy. You have inspired me, beloved, to write this prayer:

Father, you call us to shout for joy but our hearts are burdened, our spirits are weary and our hands are heavy. The root of bitterness grows deep within. We find it hard at times to give or to receive love. We have been hurt by others, in our schools and places of recreation, by those we had loved and trusted. We have been made to feel inadequate, unable to cope, unwanted. Renew us in your love.

Lord, we have wasted our years, the locusts have devoured our harvests. Stretch forth your hand and renew us, and restore what the locusts have eaten. Reach out and touch our past, Lord, so that we may live in the present and not be afraid of the future. Renew us in your love.

Sing over us, Lord, as at festivals. Sing to us as you sang to Mary at the dawn of the New Creation. We claim this promise, that you would renew us in your love. Sing to us the love-song that Mary heard: Rejoice ... the Lord is with you.

Believe me if ...

Beloved,

Loving you is not a matter of duty, though indeed in the best sense of the word, I regard it as one of my most sacred tasks in life to take your wishes into consideration. But let me say right away, that the Creator of truth and beauty has seen fit to give me a companion who is most suited to my dreams and desires. In my eyes, you are all fair, and with the author of the Song of Songs, I say, let me see your face. Every encounter with you is a royal visitation, like that of Mary to her country cousin. Like Elizabeth I hear your voice and my heart leaps for joy.

But what I want you to know is that my love for you goes deeper than the vision of the eye and the sound in the ear. It is not your appearance or any of your lovely touches that draw me and keep me faithful to our covenant. The essence of covenant as found in sacred scripture is grounded in loving kindness and fidelity. Beauty can fade like the rose, but love is stronger than death.

I'm reminded of one of the greatest love stories ever told, that of Thomas Moore, the nineteenth century Irish poet. He returned one time after lengthy business to find not his beautiful bride but the family doctor. His wife had contracted smallpox and the disease had left her once flawless skin pocked and scarred. Having seen her reflection, she commanded that the shutters be drawn, and that her husband never see her again.

Moore would not listen, ran upstairs and entered the darkness of his wife's room. He went to light the gas lamps, but heard a startled cry; 'No! Don't light the lamps!' Moore hesitated, swayed by the pleading in the voice. 'Go!' she begged. 'Please go! This is the greatest gift I can give you now.'

Moore did go, but to his study where he sat up most of the night prayerfully writing. It was not a poem this time, but a song for the first time ever. The next morning he returned to his wife's room, felt his way to a chair and sat down. He sang to his young wife the song he had written for her:

Believe me, if all those endearing young charms,
Which I gaze on so fondly today.
Were to change by tomorrow and flee from my arms,
Like fairy gifts fading away.
Thou wouldst still be adored, as this moment thou art.
Let thy loveliness fade as it will –
And around the dear ruin, each wish of my heart
Would entwine itself verdantly still.

The song ended. Moore heard his bride rise, cross the room to the window, reach up and slowly draw open the shutters.

Beloved, I read an old saying once that said, *If our souls had windows, what a demand there would be for shutters.* I want to tell you something, my dearest. Neither you nor I have need of shutters, for we love openly before the light of God's face.

Prometheus, who broke ranks

Beloved,

The life of grace, or maybe I should just say the graced relationship which we share, does not take away any of our lovely
human ways. It does of course demand that we keep a watchful
eye on our frailty and look to the Lord as our strength and salvation. The song that we sing is new. It is also as old as the hills
and as universal as the whole human race. While Jesus came to
cast the fire of divine love on the earth, he would have been
aware of the longing for love that is instinctive to every creature.

There is a powerful story from the world of the old Greek
gods about how one of them took pity on humanity as it lay
frozen in a loveless Winterland. Heathen people lived in fear of
their gods who inhabited every stream and river and tree and
valley and every natural force. Each of this collection of deities
had to be placated and cajoled. As a result, religion was more of
a hindrance than a help.

Prometheus, however, was moved to pity for humans. He
seems to have broken ranks with the establishment of the gods,
who were a jealous and grudging lot in their dealings with the
human race. It was in the cold comfortless days before human
beings possessed the gift of fire. They shivered in winter and
they had difficulty in cooking food or providing energy. Out of
compassion, Prometheus took fire from heaven and gave it as
pure gift to the world.

Zeus, the chief of the gods was angry at this gesture and
chained Prometheus to a rock in the Adriatic Sea. By day, he was
tortured from the burning sun and by night from the cold. A
vulture tore out his liver every day, but it grew by night, only to
be ripped out again. Such was the treatment meted out to a god
who tried to help the human race. The gods were a selfish cartel,
jealous and vengeful and in no way wanting to share with the
creatures of earth.

Far from this jealousy and reluctance to share, our God wants us to be partakers of his divine nature. The flame of divine love is not encased or enclosed. It is a wild fire that cannot be stopped in its consuming embrace. At the same time, it is a kindly fire like the fire we gather round as a family on a cold night. It makes us children of the heavenly father.

There is a delightful story of a Roman Emperor returning to the city after success in battle. He rides in his chariot with his trophies of war and with his generals up to the triumphal arch. On the sidewalks, the citizens of Rome acclaim his victories with loud cheers. At one stage in the grand march, a small boy breaks through the barriers and runs towards the Emperor's chariot. The great strong Legionaries tried to force him back shouting: 'What do you think you're doing rushing at the Emperor?'

The lad laughs and replies, 'He may be your Emperor, but he is my Father.' The lad had come with his mother to welcome home his dad!

What a difference it made to know he was a precious son! Thanks to the victory of the cross, beloved, you and I can join the victory parade, and have the privilege of calling God, Father.

This Golden chain and locket

Beloved,

I'm sending you a token to remind you of how I endeavour to safeguard our union in the heart of Jesus. It is this simple chain with a locket attached in the form of a golden heart. Inside the metal heart, you will find a picture of the united hearts of Jesus and Mary. You say, I have been Jesus for you, and you know that I have always found the face of Mary in the radiance of your being.

I asked the jeweller to place twelve ruby stones in the chain to stand for the Lord's prayer, the ten Hail Marys and the final Glory be of each decade of the Rosary. The Rosary that I say is a living Rosary, for we are living stones forming one building for the glory of God. The mysteries are filled out in our own flesh. I find details of your life and of so many other lives, hidden in the various mysteries. So I don't live in the past with a Jesus of yesterday.

Once when talking about the Rosary, a young Dublin working man challenged me. 'The trouble with Jesus Christ,' he said 'is that he's dead. What the lads that work down here want, is a Saviour alive today, like Big Jim Larkin, who organised them into a trade union to fight for their rights.'

I did my best at the time to explain that, unlike the Eastern meditation that was then coming on stream, we were not just emptying our minds of everything. We were reaching out to a Christ and his Mother who were alive today. Meditation such as we have in the Rosary, keeps us in touch with reality, the Christian reality which holds all things in being, and is the real and lasting stuff of life.

At one time, I found the Rosary a difficult prayer, but that encounter with the young Dublin docker changed things. I began to struggle with the fact that the mysteries of Jesus were not merely events of the past. Jesus is alive today and his mysteries are not just scenes to be remembered and thought about in the head. They pack power for now. The Rosary with its mysteries, I discovered, was no longer a wearisome repetition. It became a simple and effective way of channelling unlimited power to my own life.

Attention is relative to the measure of personal interest. So when we see the Christ events as touching ourselves and being part of what we are called to be, it becomes easy to find rest in them.

Beloved, when we say the Rosary together, we think of our calling to Divine love. Together we share in the mystery of Annunciation. Your coming to me, has been a Visitation and you bring me the Christ that you carry within you. We have our own Agony and Crucifixion. But we have the blessed hope of Resurrection and Ascension when we will forever sing and dance with the whole court of heaven. With the Rosary, we align ourselves to the life, death and glory of Jesus, so that nothing of our life, our labour and our love is be lost, but yields a harvest of eternal life and love.

Wear this golden chain and locket, beloved, and remember that you hold the key to the hearts of Jesus and Mary. It is the key to our own hearts too.

The History of my heart

Beloved,

I cannot tell you the history of my heart unless I share with you something of the journey which for fifty years took me all over the roads of Ireland and Great Britain where I have many precious friends and lovely memories. All these have been joined together by the golden chain of the Rosary. They form indeed a living Rosary and one sweet mystery of life.

The Rosary is not just something I say. It is something I have become. Blessed and beautiful as the beads are, they only come alive when used by those who believe and love. The mysteries viewed as events of two thousand years ago, are past history. They become life-giving present mysteries only when we make them our own. We have to lay hold of them in our personal lives. I think this is what the poet had in mind when he wrote those lovely lines:

> Sweet blessed beads,
> I would not part with one of you,
> for richest gem that gleams in kingly diadem.
> Ye know the history of my heart.

The *Annunciation* mystery is my first morning prayer. Like Mary, I wait for God's message for this day. I try to answer: Be it done to me according to your word. It is exciting wondering what may turn up. The Word has to become flesh for me today.

In the *Visitation*, I pray: O Mary visit me this day as you visited Elizabeth. When God and his Blessed Mother are with us, beloved, every day becomes a Cana day. Mary watches out for every need and notices if the wine of joy and gladness may be running out.

For the *Nativity*, I alternate between asking Mary to bring me Jesus and wondering how I may bring him to birth in others. Every day is a birthday as our Christ-life reaches a new stage of growth.

In the *Presentation*, I think of the old man in the Temple proclaiming Jesus as the Light of the nations, and I trust that no act of mine, may hinder the light of Christ from shining through. I ask Mary and Joseph to carry me to God's temple and make me presentable to God and presentable to you, my beloved.

What I like about the *Finding in the Temple* is the bit where Jesus is sitting among the wise old men listening to them and asking them questions. I ask the Father to make us temples of the divine presence, and let his Son sit beside us to listen to our needs and to search our hearts with his questions.

My comfort in any personal *Agony* is to walk in the garden or along the streets, thinking of Jesus who sweated blood beneath the green olives of Gethsemene. There, I pray for courage, to take my share in the agony of our times.

For the *Scourging at the Pillar*, I ask Jesus to use the sufferings of life as a means of healing, remembering the words of the Prophet, *By his wounds, we are healed*. In this way nothing is lost. Even the trials and tribulations of daily living work unto eternal life.

At the *Crowning with Thorns* I look at the Claddagh ring which you, beloved, gave me. I note the two hands holding the heart and the crown overhead, and I pray: 'O Jesus, my heart is in your hands. You are King of my life.'

The *Carrying of the Cross* conjures up the Saviour struggling through the narrow streets of Jerusalem. From there, I see a long line stretching through the bloodied streets of war-torn lands and through all those areas of disaster and devastation that light up our television screens. Past history becomes living mystery and we are all caught up in it.

In the *Crucifixion* I behold the dying Saviour and think of my own death. This is something I want you to recall, if and when, beloved, I go home before you. I do not wish you to grieve much over me, as I want to make my death an offering, as Jesus did. I desire this to be the supreme moment of surrender into the hands of a loving Father. We must not miss the glory of this moment. Whether you be near or far at the time, I would simply wish you to stand in spirit with me, as Mary stood beside the Cross.

The *Resurrection* and the *Ascension* give direction to all our struggles and wanderings. At times we get lost. Again I run ahead of myself. But this I'm sure of: we know where we're going. We're heading for the place Jesus has prepared for us. There we will be home at last.

Meanwhile we want all the graces and gifts the *Holy Spirit* has in store. We're tempted to go it alone, to live out of our own meagre ration, instead of relying on God's infinite supply. Send forth your Spirit, O Lord, and renew the face of the earth. Renew what is old and stale. Restore the lost years and put a new heart within us.

In the glorious *Assumption* of Mary into heaven, as I near the end of my Rosary journey, I picture the Blessed Mother at the window of heaven, calling: 'Arise my love, my dove, my beautiful one and come. The flowers have appeared in our land. The time for singing has come.'

As I look to you, beloved, as my queen on earth, I see you as the image of the heavenly Queen. She is the icon who enshrines within herself, the little lives of us all. The graces bestowed on her are unique, yet in a sense shared by all. Her *Coronation* inspires every believer to work in the service of Jesus, her Son, who is Lord and King.

The Mysteries of Light

Beloved

I have a weakness for stories about little creatures being changed into big strong beings. As for fairytales about frogs that emerge as handsome princes, and swans that turn into lovely ladies, they seem to say something very deep to me. Little children love to have these stories told to them at bedtime. Not only do they rest in them, they fall blissfully asleep as they are read aloud at bedtime. These transformation stories speak to every heart that longs for change, or that seeks a lift to higher ways.

One of my favourites is about the princess who lets her golden ball fall into the lake, only to have it rescued by a frog. The frog makes this request: 'I want to sit beside you at the King's table. I want to eat from your own golden plate. Then I want you to put me asleep on a silk cushion beside your bed. In the morning you must wake me with a kiss on the forehead.' You already know, beloved, how the story ends. The wicked spell is broken and there stands a splendid prince, and they live happily ever after.

We all long for the healing kiss of love. In the Christian order, we are destined to be kissed and transformed into the likeness of Jesus. We are all called to be princes and princesses of the Royal Blood of the Saviour, and to sit at his banquet table of the Eucharist. What has brought all this to my mind is the introduction of the new *Mysteries of Light* in the Rosary.

The Baptism of Jesus reminds us that we are all called and chosen to be beloved sons and daughters of the Father. A voice came from heaven saying, 'This is my Son, the Beloved.' That voice is the kiss of life for each one of us.

The Marriage Feast of Cana is our invitation to what the Book of Revelation calls, the wedding of the Lamb. We are not only children of God. We are invited to be in a spousal relationship with him. From this bond there arises the security of knowing that we are not mere casual labourers in the vineyard. We have the standing of being in a covenant relationship with the King.

The Proclamation of the Kingdom means that we are no longer in the dark pool of despair and depression, but that we are people of the Light. We are called to walk in the radiance of divine light, and to be sources of light and love for others who still walk in the valley of darkness.

The Transfiguration mystery most of all, speaks of the innate desire of the human heart for a higher way of life. Not just Peter, James and John are called to climb the mountain. All of us are to be mountain climbers. We dare not settle for the mediocrity and half measures of the misty flats. The poet John Oxenham has inspired many to climb out of the mists and walk the higher way of genuine Christian living:

> To every man there openeth
> A way, and ways and a way.
> And the high soul climbs the high way,
> And the low soul gropes the low,
> And in between, on the misty flats,
> The rest drift to and fro.
> And to every man there openeth
> A high way and a low,
> And every man decideth the way his soul shall go.

You and I are not meant to drift and grope our way through the mists. We are invited to climb the high mountain of light and share something of the glory of the Lord. We pray: 'Take us with you, Lord and transfigure us. By your grace, help us to yield to the glory you have destined for us.'

The final mystery of the *Blessed Eucharist* is a summons from the King, to sit at his table and be nourished from the golden plate of eternal life, and to drink from the cup of the new and everlasting covenant.

Beloved, let the child in us go on reading the fairy stories of lowly creatures raised to a new life. But let our souls go deeper, as we are share in the divine transfiguration at work within us. Washed in the Precious Blood of Jesus, we walk with the dignity of new creatures into the land of light.

Slow me down, Lord

Beloved,

I'm sorry to learn that you were hit with a flying brick, by one of your so-called friends. You say it happened when you were rushing on an errand of mercy and did not have time to stop and state your case. Now the whole thing has built up and is festering.

Welcome to the club! It happens all the time. One of the Psalms talks about how terrible it would be if an enemy had done this. But this came about through one who prays and plays with you and says nice things to your face.

Reminds me of the young man who was tearing down the street in his flashy new car. He was on the watch for children darting out from the footpath. As he raced ahead, a brick hurtled into the door. He slammed on the brakes and stopped the car at the spot from where the brick had come. In a rage, the driver jumped out, grabbed the first child, pushed him against a wall and yelled, 'What in hell's bells are you up to? Look at the damage you've done to my car.'

Tears streamed down the boy's eyes as he blurted out, 'I threw the brick because no one looked or listened to my cry.' Pointing to the road, he said, 'That's my brother. He slipped off the path and fell into the road in his wheel chair. I was not able to lift him up.' In piteous tones the little boy begged for help.

Seeing the brother bleeding on the road, the driver's heart repented. He helped the handicapped lad into his wheel chair, got someone to wipe the wound clean, and called the nearest ambulance. Still in a state of shock, the little boy mumbled 'Thank you.'

The driver walked back to his new car, now badly damaged. He never had that door mended. He left the dent as it was, to remind him to live with eyes open and ears alert. Never again would someone have to throw a brick at him to remind him to slow down.

God meets us in strange ways. His voice is gentle and we need to be on the alert. Often we are too busy. We do not have time to listen. Someone has to throw a brick at us.

Beloved, the brick that caught you in the back, when you were in a rush, may well have been a message. The best thing I can suggest is that you take a leaf out of St Paul's letter to the Corinthians, when he begins his piece on charity, by saying *Love is patient*. Before all the other glowing tributes to love, he set down patience top of the list.

Have you heard about the two mice that fell into a tub of cream? One looked at the slippery side of the tub, and reckoned that it was too high up. 'Hopeless,' he cried, and resigned himself to death. He closed his eyes and sank to the bottom.

The second mouse kept treading the cream with every breath he had left. He kept kicking out and churning away at the cream, the way he had seen the farmer's wife churning the cream in the dairy.

What do you think happened? The mouse that refused to give up found itself on a solid platform of butter and jumped to safety.

Patient expectation is no stick-in-the-mud. It just never gives up. Patience, like every virtue, lies between two extremes. On the one hand is the vice of being impetuous and intolerant, never satisfied with how things are done. On the other extreme, is the vice of being so unconcerned that one just stagnates. Patience like the mouse had, treads the middle ground. Those who practise patience, live and move in the Spirit and are sweetly attuned to the Divine timing.

So, beloved, I want you to forgive, and be patient with yourself. You are still part of God's unfinished business. You say you were rushing. I'm afraid that this is one of my own failures. You tell me that I seem to be living in tomorrow land and that in my rush to reach the stars, I trample the wild flowers in my path. One thing I know is that I often fail to respect your rhythms. I try to hurry you up and, in the process, the peace and calm that should be in our souls and in our bodies is broken .

This is a lesson I have to learn over and over again; that a woman is like a bird in her nest. She must be given the time that nature demands. God's timing is a delicate balance somewhere between dead-slow and hurry-up! Please forgive, beloved, my own undue haste.

Stop flirting – Start loving

Beloved,

They say that a man likes to think that the woman in his life is his first love. The woman likes to think that he has met his last love. However that may be, one thing we know is that God must be our first and our final love, as he leads us in strange paths, in ways that we know not. I cling to the lines in the canticle of Isaiah, 'I will lead the blind in ways that they know not; in paths that they have not known. I will guide them. I will turn the darkness before them into light, the rough places into level ground.'

One thing I know, beloved, is that when God brought our pathways together, I found a stability and security that brought my wandering and wavering to a resting place. I stopped flirting with life and with the lives of others and settled down to the tranquillity of order that brought peace to my soul and body. When there is nothing and no one special to anchor the soul, it is easy to flirt with everyone and everything, and lead an elusive butterfly existence oneself.

How often as a priest hearing confessions, I have listened to struggling fellow-butterflies saying, *Forgive me, father, but I promise, I'll never see her again. I'll ask the bishop to move me to the other end of the diocese.*

Can this be the answer to anything? Meeting up with someone for a passing few days and then walking away. How does the other party feel? Maybe they have a good conscience and have a noble purpose. How do they feel? After all, it is a two-sided situation.

Have I the right to win the affections of another and then when things get messy, turn my back on them? I may have a wooden heart, but can I treat the other as if she were equally wooden?

I can find myself saying to a penitent, 'You may have to call things gently to an end. You may not be able to handle this. It may not be God's time for the gift he has in store for you.'

Or I may have to make a prudential judgement and say: 'Walk out in faith, one step at a time in grace. Don't panic. Don't run away. You have to stop running around and running away from life. Stop flirting with all and sundry. Stop the illusions and the images and face a real live woman, the total person with all that goes with her. Good women are for real and they lead you true. Fancy women of idle dreaming are the ones that keep you running over the hills and getting nowhere.'

Needless to say, we can all make mistakes and the celibate is no more free from danger than anyone else. However, I like the expression of Raisa Maritain, *Adventures in grace*. Keep you eyes on Jesus, be faithful to your time before the tabernacle. Walk with Rosary in your hands. Be alert to your adventure in grace.

Beloved, you and I must watch for winter to be over, so that the flowers may bloom in our land. Remember the song I sang for you last Christmas, *Keep a green bough in your heart and God will send a singing bird.*

Alone with the great alone

Beloved,

You and I both know that there are times for being alone with the great Alone. Solitude and silence are essentials of our lives. We have little to give to others until we have found stability and rest in ourselves. We need to stand alone with God, before we can reach out to others. Our relationship is a mutual exchange, a giving and receiving. But what we give, beloved, is not our own poor hearts, but ourselves already steeped in the riches of the Heart of Jesus.

The celibate runs the risk of remaining locked in a sanctity of self-sufficiency, seemingly rich, yet trapped in a self-inflicted poverty. Genuine love is the key that unlocks the trap and allows us to open our treasure-chest to another.

You helped me find the key, the golden key of love, that frees me from selfishness and makes me live for the other. I rejoice in your glory more than in my own. You show me how to place my foot on the first step to the glory of God. Nothing pleases me more than to see you smile and know that you are happy, and that in this shared happiness we know a little of the smile of heaven. Without someone and something like this, solitude becomes sterile and silence smells of the graveyard.

Before writing to you today, I sat alone with Jesus in the Blessed Sacrament, exposed here in our oratory. I never cease to marvel at the priestly grace of changing the little white circle of bread into the food of eternal life. We want to be spiritually strong to care for each other, and I asked the Lord to nourish us with this bread of angels.

Even as I sat alone, I thought of the bond that binds us in a covenant of love. We are not married as husband and wife in the ordinary sense, but we are married in the highest and best sense, and the Eucharist is our wedding banquet. Our marriage feast is not an affair of a day. We celebrate it every day as we receive the Blessed Eucharist and kneel in adoration before this Blessed Sacrament.

When I stood up to go, I lifted the little monstrance and turned with it outwards towards the window, for I want our eucharistic union to be the window through which we look out on the world. I asked the Lord to bless all those entrusted to our care, and prayed that he would make us instruments of his healing love.

Going home

Beloved,

I spent some time with a farmer last Autumn helping to stack the wheaten stalks. As the evening sun was setting, he glanced back over the new mown field and said, 'I planted the seed last spring and it lay under the earth without a human hand to touch it. The corn and the straw will be there to get the cattle through the winter. Now we're heading home and isn't it a grand thing to have a home to go to.'

As the autumn of life is leading on to winter for myself, beloved, my mind often turns to the fact that soon I should be going home for good. I say for good, because I don't want you to be saddened at my departure. One of my earlier letters referred to the book by a fellow Dominican, *To Heaven with Diana*. Our union rests on the foundation that we are both abandoned to divine providence. While our feet are planted firmly in the earth and while we value the good things that the Lord has given us in this world, our eyes are always fixed on the heavenly things.

Heaven is being at home with God, yet we are already halfway there. The amazing thing is that Jesus has already made his home among us and continues to move in our midst. He said, 'If any one loves me, he will keep my word, and my Father will love him and we will come and make our home with him.' That's a fantastic promise and we need to claim it for ourselves here and now. As that text shows, heaven begins on earth. That's why grace is called the Seed of Glory.

Most likely, I'll have gathered up the wheaten stalks before your turn comes, but as you look over the autumn fields, you might recall the words of the Divine Office:

> O Godhead, here untouched, unseen,
> All things created bear your trace.
> The seed of glory sown in man,
> Will flower when we see your face.

Of course there is sadness and evil in our world. But those who cherish that seed of glory know that while the spring seed lies in the damp earth, it will one day bring forth an autumnal glory. The truth and goodness, justice, love and peace that we share, will never die.

The moments of happiness we have experienced together will not be lost. Times of achievement, or quieter times when we were close and tender, will come to full bloom in heaven. Fleeting moments that yielded their little joys, will be extended beyond the borders of time and space. One day we will hold infinity in our hands and we will taste eternity in the company of our God.

How I long to share this unending joy with you, beloved, when all tears will be wiped away and our lowly bodies and our little worth will be transformed. We will play in the hills of heaven and know the splendour of transfiguration.

> Eternal Father, loving God,
> Who made us from the dust of earth,
> Transform us by the Spirit's grace,
> Give value to our little worth.

The wonder is that we are not waiting listlessly around for all this to happen. With the seed of glory already planted in our souls, heaven is already among us. As Catherine of Siena remarked, all the way to heaven, is heaven too. So let's give heaven entry now and learn to enjoy God and each other as we gather up the sheaves.

Up to the time of Jesus, death was considered the end of everything. There was no hope beyond the grave. Whatever belief the Jews had about the afterlife, it did not seem very hopeful. It was Jesus who changed all that by opening up the hope of a personal and glorious life in the next world.

The unbeliever sees death as farewell forever to home, to spouse and children. The thought is unbearable. How awful to think of separation forever from all that is good and true and beautiful. What tragedy never to see parents, children or spouse again.

Faith tells us that these things find their fulfilment in the God who created them. The little lights of this life will not go out with the last candle. They will just grow and glow in a new and trans-formed splendour. The poet Alfred Lord Tennyson, thinking about death, wrote these lines:

> Our little systems have their day,
> They have their day and cease to be.
> They are but broken lights of Thee
> And Thou, O Lord art more than they.

Lift up your heart then, beloved, for when the darkness is over, we will walk in unending light and love forever beneath the shining sun of heaven.

All things bright and beautiful

Beloved,

I purred with delight over your story about Beauty, your cat. Do you know about the old Irish monk who had a white cat called Pangur Bán, who kept him company in his hermitage and helped him to settle in to study and contemplation? If I come across the poem he wrote about Pangur, I'll send it to you.

Dominicans have always loved animals. It must be part of our original interest in the goodness of creation, when we had to face the dark pessimism of the Cathars who denied the goodness of earthly and bodily things.

To return to your Black Beauty, I quote from your letter in the hope that others may profit by your experience:

He just walked in, through the gate, up the path, and onto my lap. His fur was full of all kinds of undergrowth. I was completely taken by surprise. He just lay there contentedly while I sorted him out. After about an hour he got up and off he went, round the corner and down the road. My eyes followed him and I reflected that he seemed a very special cat, but then I thought little more about him.

August gave way to September, when he appeared again. This time he refused to go. I told him to go home. He pretended not to hear. I gave him a saucer of milk outside the back door! Still he refused to move. I called the Cats' Protection League who begged me to keep him for just a few days as they had no foster home available. Of course that was fatal. He was in and that was that. I started reading all the cat books I could lay my hands on. If I was to be his mum I wanted to do it properly! That was four years ago.

Beauty has taught me a lot. For one thing, patience. He is never in a hurry. He watches, waits, washes, and finally acts. What a discernment process he exhibits. While I rush around and fuss, he sits still. He is a born contemplative, always sitting and looking. He reminds me of the beauty, joy and necessity of contemplation. More often than not we do it together.

At any time of the day he will hop on to my lap, politely requesting that I leave aside whatever I am doing and give him my full attention. I almost never refuse to do this. And so we sit together, he purring, I stroking, enabling me to turn naturally to prayer. There he lies, so totally trusting, a perfect image of oneself in God's hands. He is so fragile, so utterly dependent on human kindness, as we are on our God. I wonder how anyone could harm any of these little ones or any part of God's creation. I feel very privileged that he chose me to spend his life with.

Thanks, beloved, for sharing your story. I too want to be kind to animals for I believe they are God's silent creatures. Of course they have a sign language of their own. When I meet dogs in the park or on the street, I stop to greet them. Their eyes light up and they seem to brighten my day. I am saddened by poor dogs with their tails down between their legs, but I leap for joy when their tails go up and around with delight. They seem to need our company and I reckon that that must be something the good Lord has put into their nature. Do you know that doctors have discovered that people with pets live longer, stay healthier, recover faster and experience less depression?

When I see a pretty pussy or a happy dog, I pray, along the lines of the Mass offering: *Blessed are you Lord, God of all creation. Through your goodness we have this lovely creature.*

Have you noticed how the cattle in the field move over to the hedge and gaze at you curiously, when you stop to look at them. It is as if they knew the Pauline doctrine of the entire creation groaning in expectation of the new creation in Jesus.

The original curse that came on creation at the fall of Adam and Eve, is to be replaced with the blessing of the Saviour. The eyes of the cattle are pools of pity and patience, as if crying to every passer-by, 'Are you one of those adopted children of God for whom we are waiting for our bodies to be set free?' (Cf Rom 8:2-23)

God loves animals. How we treat them reveals a lot about our character. A man wrote to a hotel in Florida where he wanted to go for vacation, and asked, 'Could I bring my dog with me? He's very well behaved.' The hotel owner replied, 'I've been operating this hotel for years, and in all that time I've never had a dog steal towels, bedclothes, silverware or pictures off the walls. I've never had to evict a dog in the middle of the night for being drunk and disorderly. I've never had a dog run out without paying the bill. Yes, indeed, your dog is welcome at my hotel and, if your dog will vouch for you, you're welcome to stay here too!'

Beloved, if you turn up with your cat at my place, know that you are both more than welcome.

How do I love you?

Beloved,

I have already told you that our love must be such that its full flowering will be in heaven. I came across a poem by Elizabeth Browning which ends with the line, *I shall love thee better after death.* It is the message of St Dominic who assured his children that he would be more helpful to them after he had died than when he was alive. It is the message of the Little Flower who promised to shower down roses on those who remained on earth.

Elizabeth Barrett Browning was the famous poet of Victorian England. During her life time she was more admired than her husband Robert. Her romance with him brought out much of the delicate sweetness of her poetry, as is clear from the poem, *How do I love thee?*

> How do I love thee?
> Let me count the ways.
> I love thee to the depth and breadth and height
> My soul can reach,
> When feeling out of sight.
> For the ends of Being and ideal grace.
>
> I love thee to the level of everyday's
> Most quiet need;
> By sun and candlelight.
> I love thee freely,
> As men strive for right;
>
> I love thee purely,
> As they turn from praise.
> I love thee with the passion put to use
> In my old griefs, and
> With my childhood's faith.

I love thee with a love I seemed to lose
With my lost saints,
I love thee with the breath,
Smiles, tears, of all my life!
And if God choose,
I shall love thee better after death.

Elizabeth injured her spine in a fall at the age of sixteen. Her condition was aggravated by the shock of her brother's drowning in 1838, and she became an invalid. She spent most of her time in a darkened room, where she wrote poetry and many letters.

You sometimes tell me, beloved, that you are afraid of death. I suppose that is only natural. But then death is the gateway to a whole existence that is way beyond the realm of the natural.

I remember a film about the evangelist, Peter Marshall, who was comforting his little son because of a similar fear. 'Son,' he said, 'you know how Mammy puts you to sleep in the back-room where it is quiet and dark. During the night, she moves you to the nursery at the front of the house. When you wake, the sun is streaming in through the window and you are all aglow and you run outside. Dying is a bit like that. You lie down in the dark and fall asleep. When you wake, you will be playing in the streets of heaven and the sun will be forever shining.'

Let us make haste, beloved, to the sunshine.

Late have I loved you

Beloved,

I heard a man on his deathbed say to his wife: 'I never did you justice. For fifty years you've put up with me, and I never did you justice!' I thought of that beautiful line from St Augustine: *Late have I loved you … long have I sought Love outside, but you were within me, and I was not with you.* I trust that our love mirrors that loving and longing that found its way into the soul of Augustine.

So few stop to think deeply about love. I don't mean the sort of love depicted on much of TV or in trashy novels. I mean real love that endures, whether the beloved is absent or present. The love that makes my heart bleed because you are suffering. The love of God for me and for you, the love that often hurts.

No one can measure love or hold it in a jar. In our weak human nature we're not capable of loving any but ourselves. It is only when we think of God's love that we begin to see things clearly. He does not separate his love for us from our everyday lives, but demonstrates this love through each one of us. It is his Spirit that draws us above our human nature and helps us to really love our neighbour as ourselves.

What we thought was love: *Don't go – I can't live without you;* or *If you love me you'll do as I say,* is not love. It is self-indulgence. That's loving a person for my own sake. Or, indeed, if we love someone for their sake: *I love her because she's gentle and kind and sweet* – that can't be love either, because as soon as I discover that she's really bad-tempered and selfish and sour I'll stop loving her.

True love can only come from God. The man who loves his neighbour must above all else love God first. 'If you really love me,' the Lord said to his weeping disciples, 'you would rejoice because I go to the Father.' Real love seeks only the good of the beloved, at whatever cost to oneself. It's not in our nature to love one another so unselfishly, but God, if we let him, can love others with our heart. He can warm, with his heart, our hearts of clay and teach us how to love one another as we ought.

Beloved, this is the love which makes us want to do things for each other simply for love of God. When our love is centred on God, it is he who loves you, not me, and your love for me is really his love for me. However, when Jesus said: 'Love one another as I have loved you,' I don't think he meant that we must all go out and get ourselves crucified, rather that we should love each other in him.

In his love, for instance, we can recognise each other's faults, and love each other anyway. 'Give me your sins,' he said to St Anthony. His unfathomable love for us, sinners that we are, is so intense that he wants us to give him the burden of our guilt and sin, so that we will be free to dance and sing and joy in his love.

They say that in a truly happy marriage, a man and his wife end up thinking as one, even quite often beginning to look like one another! It's a fusion of souls. This love transcends the boundary of sex, explaining the deep love which often exists between friends. This is the love of Jesus for Lazarus and his sisters, and of John for Jesus. Our Blessed Lady and St Joseph obviously entered their marriage with this knowledge of God's love. Most of us are on our deathbeds before we realise it.

I would imagine that there would be no point in learning to love each other as Christ loves us, if we did not express or demonstrate our love for each other. I always thought there was something terribly sad about that lovely song by Handel called *Silent Worship*.

> Did you not see my lady,
> Go down the garden singing?
> Blackbird and thrush were silent
> To hear her sweet voice ringing.
> Ah, surely you saw my lady
> Out in the garden there;
> Shaming the rose and lily,
> For she is twice as fair.

Silent worship! What a pity to write such a song, and remain in silent worship! Maybe the lady went to her grave not knowing how much that poor poet loved her.

So, beloved, I write these lines to you to let you know that I cannot remain silent, but tell you to your face and before the face of God, that I worship you and that at the sound of your ringing voice, my heart leaps for joy.

I'm no longer the centre

Beloved,

Copernicus turned things upside down and inside out for many, by declaring that this world was not the centre of things, but was simply orbiting round the sun, which was at the heart of the matter. Beloved, you have brought about a Copernican revolution in my life.

It came as a traumatic experience to discover that I was not as important as I had been thinking. I have had to face the truth that I am not the central character on life's stage. I am not the one round which everything revolves. The way I had been living the celibate life, was not what I now see as God's way. I'd been seeing people and situations merely as they impinged on my life. I had them classified as to how they compared with myself and how they affected my position. For too long I had been in love with my own importance. In my own eyes, I have been a little sun around which others seemed to gravitate.

We all need a centre, a resting place from which to reach out. But where is it, or who is it? At certain critical points or at times of silence and reflection, I would have sensed the Lord saying: 'You are not the centre of anything – at least not anymore. So let go, and let me step right into the centre of your being.'

St Paul assured me that Christ Jesus is the one in whom 'we live and move and have our being'. He is the centre in whom all things hold together. Without this holding centre, we fall apart and our world falls apart. This is a wholesome message for all who suffer from darkness and depression.

I know, however, beloved, that I needed all you brought, to assure me that I was loveable, loveable in your eyes and in God's eyes. The theology books filled my head with the articles and theses on charity. They told me all the divisions and distinctions of grace. It simply left me cold as it was served up on ice.

Only when I experienced love made flesh in you, did the ice melt and my life take fire. You touched my soul and fired my heart. Filled with the Holy Spirit, you taught me how to place Christ in glory at the centre of my being. I found a centre, a resting place. Stability and direction followed. I ceased running round in circles after the latest fashion and folly. No longer fragmented, torn this way and that, I came to move in the Spirit around Jesus, my centre.

I hear you calling me to this centre where I find the depth of God and the depth of your soul mingling like two rivers of living water:

> Deep is calling on deep, in the roar of waters.
> Your torrents and all your waves sweep over me.
> (Psalm41)

Give me a break

Beloved,

You tell me that you are going through a rough patch and that the only prayer you can make is, *Lord I've had enough. Give me a break*. I must accept what you say and where you are. I wish I could do something practical to help. Of one thing I can assure you, that nothing of your loving heart will go to waste. I often find that when the going gets tough with myself, that your hidden suffering sustains me. As the song has it: *You are the wind beneath my wings*.

We all tend to cry, *Lord give me a break*, when locked into a situation where things seem hopeless, helpless, humanly impossible. I suggest that you turn to the great breakthrough story in the gospel of St John:

> The doors were closed in the room where the disciples were, for fear of the Jews. Jesus came and stood among them and said: 'Peace be with you ... As the Father sent me, so I am sending you.' He breathed upon them and said: 'Receive the Holy Spirit.'

The doors are closed, the disciples are locked in by their own fears. Suddenly there is a breakthrough. Jesus, the Lord of glory is standing in their midst. He is breathing upon them, breathing life, bestowing power.

Beloved, I pray with you and for you:

Lord Jesus, fling open the closed doors and break through the barriers and the barricades. Breathe upon me. Set me free to walk into the Easter sunlight. Come in glory and light up my darkness. Breathe on the whole, broken, bleeding situation around me. Breathe new life into my weary soul. Come and show me your life-giving, glorious wounds. Let me touch them like Thomas, and be healed. My Lord and my God!

There is a saying: God never closes one door but he opens another, and if not a door, then a window. St Paul, when hemmed in by circumstances beyond his control, prayed to be given a window of opportunity, the chance to open up a new mission for Christ. Writing to the Romans, he said that everything works for good with those who love God. (Rom 8:28)

Dr A. J. Cronin was struck down with ill health and could not continue his medical career. In the 1920s he became worn out from his work and it seemed as if his prospects were bleak indeed. He was ordered a complete rest for a year at least. What appeared a tragedy turned out to be a blessing, not only for himself but for the countless friends he made through his writing. The very first novel he wrote, *Hatters Castle*, became an instant success and has never been off the bookshelves in the years since.

The doctor, who might otherwise be forgotten, lives on in his writings and had this to say as he looked back on life: 'We cannot measure Divine Providence by the yardstick of human mentality. What we think evil may be for eventual good. God never takes without giving something in return. Disappointments and troubles are often the instruments with which he fashions us for better things to come. If we have faith, God will open a door for us, not perhaps the one that we ourselves would ever have thought of, but one which will ultimately prove good for us.'

You tell me, beloved, that you had been dreaming of a whole new future for yourself, but that it is now turning into a nightmare. Let me tell you of a certain man who let go of his dream and devoted himself to the dreams of another.

W. McKinley Smiley Junior had been told that he had cancer and could not expect to live much longer. His much-loved wife was expecting a baby and there were many things young Smiley had hoped to tell the yet unborn child. He wanted to let the baby know something of his dreams and of the hopes he had for her future. He invested in a tape recorder and set down several messages that she might listen to in the years when he would not be around to talk to her in person.

Man proposes, but God disposes! Not only did Smiley live to see his daughter Kathy grow to adulthood, but was to rejoice in the birth of a second daughter, Kristy. On Kristy's thirteenth birthday, he told the family about the messages he had recorded seventeen years earlier. As he shook the dust from the old tape he reflected on the marvel of Divine Providence that disposes as it wills: 'If you want to be truly happy,' he remarked, 'devote yourself to the fulfilment of someone else's dreams.'

Happiness, beloved, is a by-product. Aim directly for it and you may miss. But let it come as a free gift as you seek the happiness of others and it will shower you with blessings.

Have courage

Beloved,

I felt pretty low last week, but when your letter arrived, it cheered me up no end. You put new heart into me. Your story about the Italian dad, who kept saying *Corragio* to his little boy in order to pull him through the operation, reminded me of something that happened some years ago.

A famous singer was advertised to perform at the Grand Opera House in Paris. That night, the concert hall was packed with people, eager to hear her. Suddenly, the house manager went on stage and announced, 'Ladies and gentlemen, I regret that due to illness, our special guest will be unable to perform this evening. However, we've found another singer, an equally great talent, so would you please give her a warm welcome.'

The crowd groaned so loudly that nobody even heard the singer's name. You could feel the disappointment everywhere. The stand-in singer gave it everything she had, but when it was over all she got was brief, scattered applause, followed by uncomfortable silence. Suddenly, in the balcony, a child stood up and shouted, 'Mummy, I think you're wonderful!' Realising what had happened, the crowd jumped to their feet and gave the singer a standing ovation that lasted for several minutes.

Once in a while we all need to hear somebody say, 'I think you're wonderful!'

In order to encourage us in our studies, our scripture professor long ago told us to remember that the word encouragement was made up of three particles:

En which meant into

Cor which meant heart

Agere which meant to act or make to be.

In other words, beloved, encouragement means putting new heart into some one who has lost heart. You yourself did that for me. You are my Barnabas. In case you may not know what I mean by that, let me tell you about the time they were looking for a leader for the new church at Antioch. It was Barnabas, whose name means Son of Encouragement, who brought up the name of Paul, formerly known as Saul of Tarsus. Despite the revelation that had been given to Saul on the road to Damascus, and the new name bestowed on him, the other apostles had set him aside. In their eyes he was a blow-in, a Johnnie-come-late. Barnabas was the one who said, 'Let's give the man a break. I'll stand over him.'

Were it not for that encouraging word, we might never have heard much about Paul, and the letters he wrote might never have seen the light of day. When I was a boy, my dad brought home the record, *Home on the Range*. I still recall his cheery voice as he joined in and sang out the words, *Home, home on the range, where seldom is heard a discouraging word, and the skies are not cloudy all day*.

I forget the rest, but this I remember, that my dad never spoke a discouraging word. When he was around, there were no clouds in our sky. So sing and dance beloved, and thanks for all the encouraging words you have spoken to myself. They keep me happy here on this range.

Apple Blossom

Beloved,

I grew up with a small apple orchard at the back of our rented house. It was the time of World War II and things were scarce. Moreover, my dad was ill and out of work. To help out, I would climb the trees and carefully pick the fruit. Each apple was cleaned and polished and laid out in a wooden tray, lined with green moss. Next morning I would ride four miles with the boxes on the back of an ancient bicycle to the market, before attending Mass in Dublin Castle.

At the end of the season, there would be a tidy sum of money which I gladly gave to my parents, as most children would have done in those hard times. The details are pretty well faded, but the memory survives to remind me of the proverb, *God gave us memory that we might have roses in December*. My roses in this instance are the May blossoms of the apple trees. They were lavish in their profusion and perfume. Their colour and fragrance still linger to delight my senses and to heal any bitter memory.

Maybe this is why when I met you, beloved, the secret name that came to my mind was Apple Blossom. I called you that because you delighted my being and brought me healing. You were my Prophet Joel, the instrument used by divine providence to restore the years which the locusts had eaten. As blossom-time has yielded to harvest, you have borne fruit not only in our shared life, but in the lives of more than I can reckon. It reminds me of what Jesus said to his friends: 'I chose you ... to go and bear fruit, fruit that will last.' (Jn 15:16) It is the fruit of the Spirit, love, joy, peace, patience, kindness, goodness, faithfulness, gentleness and self-control. (Gal 5...22, 23) You have never left me with garbage or leftovers, but have filled life's trays with the mellow fruitfulness of your autumn giving.

Your heaped-up harvest reminds me of how one morning, when the Berlin Wall was still standing, some East Berliners came and dumped a truckload of garbage on the west side of the wall. Greatly angered, the people there thought they would return the favour, but instead they had a better idea!

They filled a truck with canned goods, medicine, clothes and other non-perishable items, then took it over to the east side. They stacked it up neatly beside the wall and put a sign near it which read, 'Each gives what he has to give!' If garbage is what you've got, garbage is what you'll give; but if love is what you've got, love is what you'll give! Love is the fruit of the Spirit, and you can bear fruit only as long as you abide in the vine.

Beloved, you are still my Apple Blossom. And if I can remember the names of the sweet apples we now get in the local green-grocer, you are my Royal Gala, and my Golden Delicious. You have never dumped garbage at my door, but laden me with fruit that will last.

Mellow fruitfulness

Beloved,

You tell me that you can't keep your mind fixed on the mysteries as you pray the Rosary. You get lost in your own dreams and anxieties.

Please forgive me for beginning with a smart remark: *Welcome to the club.* You're in good company! The plain fact is that we all have a limited span of attention. The Dominican theologian, St Thomas Aquinas says that prayer should not be unduly prolonged.

The harvest time of life weakens our capacity for detail, yet wonderfully brings us beyond meditation and concentration into the pleasant pastures of simple contemplation.

So don't be upset if you can't meditate. You may be further along the high road of prayer than you think. There is something more precious than meditation and keeping the mind fixed on a scene or situation. You may well have arrived at the land of recreative rest. With the passage of the years, there frequently comes a growth in prayer, when the soul is not so much active as blissfully restful. Call it the prayer of quiet, if you like. It is a part of your mellow autumn fruitfulness, when the strong push of rising sap and blossom has ceased, and the ripe fruit is ready for picking.

'You can't be serious', I hear you say. 'I can't find fruit in my prayer.' You are right. You can't see the fruit, but the Lord of the harvest can.

Beloved, I'm thinking of the way the May blossoms on the apple trees were tossed by the early summer wind. You are being blown along by the gentle breath of the Holy Spirit. Thomas Aquinas may well be able to help you sort out just where you are. He writes about the three degrees of attention in prayer:

      1 To the words,
      2 To the meaning,
      3 To God.

Life itself shows that growth-pattern. We begin by speaking to each other in words, and we try to choose our words carefully. We go on to talk meaningfully to each other. Finally, and best of all, we are simply there for each other. We enjoy each other's company, rest in each other's love. That's when we have passed from anxious concentration to loving regard. No need to be worried about words, or troubling the mind about what impression we're making.

So don't be worried if you forget how many Hail Marys you have said, or what mystery you began with. God knows that you are breathing in his love and that's all that matters.

God did not make you an angel, but a human being of flesh and blood. He knows that you have affairs of the world to look after, a house to keep, bills to pay, food to prepare, the doctor to see, and a whole host of other people to look after. As long as you acknowledge God as the source of all your good gifts, and have learned to hand them over to his Lordship, then there is no need to worry if these earthly concerns find their way into your prayer. And why shouldn't they? They are part and parcel of the whole package that you yourself are. It just wouldn't be you without them.

Beloved, the Lord is deeply interested in what you call your distractions. Like all true lovers, he wants to know what you're thinking, what's worrying you, so that he can solve your problems. There is a lovely song I remember from years back, which ends:

> But where do you go, my lovely,
> When you're alone in your bed?
> What are the thoughts that surround you?
> I want to see inside your head.

So many thoughts surround us, and things and more things go on inside our poor heads when we get down to prayer! But don't worry. God is well able to sort them out in his own way.

Begin your day, then, by saying: 'Here I am Lord. I am all yours, and all I have is yours. My food, my clothes, my finances, my worries, my work, my relaxation, my everything is yours, so if I come to you just as I am, I know you'll understand.'

111

And isn't it just like this, beloved, with ourselves. We have spoken the words and thought the thoughts. It is enough now that we sit together and watch in wonder, as the good Lord looks on us in love.

What's new?

Beloved,

One thing that marks you out from so many others is that you don't ply me with questions. You let things unfold, as indeed they usually do. What interests you are not things and thoughts so much as the ways of the heart and the paths of our persons.

The first remark some folk make when they meet you, is 'What's your news?' or 'What's new in your neck of the woods?'

Give my head peace. I haven't had time yet to search round the woods. In any event, I don't like sentences that begin with What? I'm rather taken by your own expression, beloved, *How about you?*

That's not so much a question, as a light-hearted remark of affection. It goes straight to my being and when I hear it from you it echoes through the halls of my heart, as the Psalm has it, *deep calling on deep.*

What has sparked this off is something I've been reading in St Paul writing to the Thessalonians. It runs: 'Like a mother feeding and looking after her children, we felt so devoted and protective towards you, and had come to love you so much, that we were eager to hand over to you, not only the good news, but our whole lives as well.'

Beloved, we write to each other and do our best to practise and preach the good news. But we want, above all, to feed and nourish each other with the life-giving word of God. We respect the individuality of each other and refrain from curious questioning. The curiosity that killed the cat is at the opposite end of the scale to the virtue of studiosity. We study each other and observe each other in love, but we never intrude. Our love is such that it respects our freedom and does not seek possession.

Edmond Holmes distinguished between this *freedom to be,* and the slavery of *possession*:

> Wilt thou be mine when death has set us free?
> Mine and mine only for evermore?

Poor earth-bound dream of love's eternity!
It's freedom, not possession, that I crave,
Freedom to love thee without let or bar,
To find new heights of love beyond the grave,
To pour forth waves of love anew, afar.

Beloved, we are not servants that we may possess or exact an account of each other. As Jesus put it, not servants but friends. In some strange way, I have never taken to the saintly Mother Teresa's expression, Co-workers. I know what she meant, and far be it from me to be critical of such a wonderful woman. Yet somehow, beloved, I could not call you a worker with me. We walk side by side, hand in hand, heart to heart. As the Acts of the Apostles has it: 'The company of those who believed were of one heart and soul …'

Growing old

Beloved,

You tell me not to be talking about getting old. You are as young as you feel! Whatever about that, I met a pensioner on the train last week, who revealed her secret of eternal youth. She was a good Belfast Presbyterian who was widowed, but believed in keeping on the move for the Lord. 'In him I live and move and have my being,' she quoted from St Paul and added, 'that counts from nine months to ninety-nine years and more.'

I can't recall the number of charitable works she is tied up with, but one thing I'll not forget, is the engaging and delightful smile that hovered over this lady's face. The light in her eyes revealed something of the inner radiance of her soul.

She handed me the small book she was reading, *Our Daily Bread*. I began to read at the page she had opened. Here's what it said: *We do not lose heart. Even though our outer nature is wasting away, our inner nature is being renewed day by day.* (2 Cor 4:16)

This is what Paul wrote to a people who lived lavishly in this world and who may well have been feeling bad as old age and ill health and latter-day misfortune bore down on them. They must have been prone to the same trials as ourselves. Knees and hips gave way to arthritic pains, and hands could no longer grip the taps and the levers of life. Dreams and desires may have yielded to the stark reality of the daily grind. They may no longer have wanted to study their faces in the mirror and wonder who was the fairest of them all.

Beloved, I want you to know that even if your features fade with the autumn, you will still be as fair in my eyes, for you hold firm to the same faith as this good lady of my train journey. Believers in the new creation of Jesus need never feel that life has passed them by.

Senior citizenship does not mean being sidelined or unproductive. In keeping with the apple trees of my youth, I try to live by the words of Psalm 92: *Those who are planted in the house of the Lord, shall still bear fruit in old age.*

Young or old, we are all being renewed from within, as we yield our lives to the Divine Harvester. Like Mary who bore the fruit of eternal life, we too carry Jesus in our hearts. In the power of the Spirit, we bring him forth, the fruit of our life, our love and our labour.

I often pray, beloved, that the Father in heaven may send his fertilising rain upon the land of our being and enable us to fill the empty fruit-bowls of those who hunger for love.

From a saintly Franciscan

Beloved,

A fellow Dominican once chided me that I was going overboard on this love business. For one thing, he said, 'It's your age! Old men like you get a bit dotty towards the end. Anyway, its best leave that to the Franciscans. They are strong on love. Our motto is truth.'

I was so taken aback by the remark that I forgot to remind my colleague that we have to *do the truth in love*. One way or another, another Dominican sent me this piece from a saintly Franciscan priest, Fr Raschi, who received it in prayer not long before his death:

I know your misery, the struggles and tribulations of your spirit, and the weaknesses of your body; I know your sins, and I tell you just the same: Give me your heart, love me as you are!

If you wait until you are an angel before abandoning yourself to love, you will never love. Even if you are negligent in doing your duty and in practising virtue, even if you continue to fall into those faults that you would like never to commit again, I refuse to allow you not to love me.

Love me as you are. At every moment and in whatever situation you find yourself, in fervour or in dryness, fidelity or infidelity, love me as you are. I wish to have the love of your poor heart. If you wait until you are perfect you will never love me. Could I not create, if I wished, out of every grain of sand, an angel radiant in purity, nobility and love? Am I not all powerful? If I should prefer to leave those wonderful beings in nothingness and prefer the poor love of your heart, am I not the dispenser of my own love? My son, my daughter, let me love you. I want your heart.

Certainly with time I want to transform you, but for now I love you as you are and I want you to do the same; I want to see love rising from the depths of misery. I love in you even your weakness, I love the love of the poor and miserable: I want a great shout to rise continually from the dust: *Jesus, I love you.*

I want only the song of your heart. I need neither your knowledge nor your talent. One thing only is important for me, to see you acting with love. It isn't your virtues that I desire. If I gave you any, you are so weak that they would increase your self-love. Do not worry about that. I could have destined you for great things. No, you will be the useless servant. I will take from you even the little that you have, because I have created you only for love.

I want you to do even the most insignificant action only for love. I am counting on you to give me joy. Do not be concerned that you have no virtues. I will give you mine.

You and I, beloved, have been drawn to each other, that we may walk this way of abandonment to divine love. We place the bread of our love in the hands of Jesus. We ask him to multiply the broken bits of our lives, in order to satisfy the hungry hearts that wait for the bread of his love.

Merciful and faithful love

Beloved,

Behind our covenant of love, lies one of the world's most beautiful stories of merciful and steadfast fidelity. It illustrates the meaning of Covenant-love, the love that lights up the pages of the Bible, and the love that lies at the heart of the Eucharist.

The story is of two young men who were rivals for power and glory, yet who remained steadfast friends. One was Jonathan, son of King Saul. The other was David, the shepherd-boy, who with a sling and a stone had slain the giant Goliath.

Although David had done valiant deeds in defence of the kingdom, Saul treated him badly. Things came to such a pass that David had to flee for his life. Jonathan realised that David was not only a good man, but that he might very well inherit the throne in due course. Between them, they made a pact that come what may, they would remain loyal to each other. They decided to make a covenant of fidelity.

A covenant is a solemn agreement, whereby not only goods are exchanged, but where there is a commitment of persons to each other. Covenants were often sealed in the blood of a sacrificial animal, or even by making a small cut on the hands, the blood of each party mingling with the other in a handshake.

Jonathan took off his princely cloak and gave it to David. This would have symbolised the merciful protection of the king's son. When people would see David so dressed, they would respect him. Moreover, Jonathan conferred on his friend his personal sword and belt.

Armed with these weapons, David could overcome his enemies and win glory for his cause. Jonathan sensed that Saul and himself would be defeated in the ensuing battle and that David would come to power. So he made this plea of mercy to one whom he now saw as the future king: 'If I am still alive, show your servant faithful love. If I die never withdraw your faithful love from my family.' Jonathan then renewed his oath to David since he loved him like his very soul.

When God wished to establish a covenant with his people, he sent his Son, so that the covenant might be sealed in his precious blood. Jesus was stripped of his royal robe that we sinners might be clothed in his love and mercy. The Spirit was given as the shining and splendid sword enabling us to overcome evil and emerge victorious.

Returning to our story: when the final battle had been fought, Saul and Jonathan were dead and David was on the throne. But the new king remembered his covenant with Jonathan and wept over his death. Remembrance and fidelity are of the essence of covenant.

Moreover, the pact that the two tribal heads had made, extended to the whole family of Saul and Jonathan. So David determined to search out any of the family of Saul that might have survived the battle. He posed the lovely question: 'Is there anyone belonging to Saul's family left, to whom I might show faithful love for Jonathan's sake?'

'There is still one of Jonathan's sons, Merribal, remaining,' he was told. 'He has crippled feet, for he fell from his nurse's arms as he was fleeing the battle.'

On entering David's presence, the boy fell at the king's feet, saying, *Here I am at your service.* But David replied: *Do not be afraid. I will indeed treat you with faithful love for your father Jonathan's sake. I shall restore all your grandfather Saul's estates to you and you will always eat at my table.* Merribal prostrated himself and said: *Who is your servant, that you show favour to a dead dog like me?*

King David then said to Ziba, an old servant of the late king Saul: 'Everything belonging to Saul and his family, I give to the boy. You must work the land for him. You must harvest and produce food for him and his family, but Merribal himself will always take his meals at my table.'

The story ends on this touching note: *Merribal lived in Jerusalem, since he always ate at the king's table. He was crippled in both feet.*

The tale, beloved, is full of eucharistic significance. It is the ground on which our own covenant table-fellowship is based. It is the charter for all Godly relationships. It holds the secret of grace which binds us together.

At the King's table

Beloved,

Though crippled in both feet, he ate always at the King's table. What a picture of merciful love! It speaks to each of us, crippled as we are in so many ways. I think not only of those deprived of the power of their limbs, but of those too who are emotionally and mentally stressed. We think of those who see themselves like Merribal, who described himself as a dead dog. There are dead-dog areas in our own lives, areas that are cut off and cannot be faced in the light of day. Covenant holds the pledge that forgiveness and healing are at hand and that the parties can sit down to break bread together.

The term covenant is allied to the expression, company, which derives from two Latin terms: *cum* which means together and *panis*, which means bread. There is a world of difference between a private snack meal and the sitting down to table eating bread together in the company of loved and loving ones. That's the kind of meal we share with the Lord and his companions at Holy Mass. No wonder St Thomas Aquinas prayed: 'O Sacred Banquet in which Christ is consumed, the memory of his passion is recalled and there is given to us, a pledge of future glory.'

In biblical times, solemn meals were eaten on the occasion of agreements or the signing of covenants. Pledges were given and the signing was marked by the shedding of blood. Normally this would be some kind of animal sacrifice. One of the Psalms says: 'Summon before me my people who have made covenant with me by sacrifice.' The people would vow fidelity and obedience to their God. They were asked to say *Yes* to the covenant and to be faithful to its terms.

In the Eucharist, that is what is meant by our saying 'Amen,' as we hear the words, 'The Body of Christ.' We are saying: 'Yes, Lord, I believe in you, I hope in you, I love you. I want to be your loyal and devoted servant. I rejoice to be called to your table and I wish to take delight in your company.'

Behind the ritual lies the reality of our covenant relationship with Jesus, and an awareness of the faithful and merciful love of his Father towards us, who are crippled by the burdens of life. We come like David to put aside our own rags and to be clothed in the princely robe of Jesus. We wear that mantle of mercy because our King has been stripped of his royal robe. We are endowed with the sword of the Spirit, only because the Prince of Glory has bowed his head and delivered up his spirit as the final gift of his covenant promise.

We come like Merribal, to have our dignity restored and to find healing. The years that the locusts have eaten are restored. The past is forgotten, our sins are blotted out. Mercy and truth have embraced and the covenant is remembered.

This is the cup of my blood. As we listen to these sacred words, beloved, let us seal our love in the blood of Jesus. We have been summoned before the face of the Lord to make covenant with him and with each other. It is good for us to be here.

Gifts in our Sleep

Beloved,

You tell me that you can't sleep, that you start thinking about the problems of the day, and it is early morning before you close your tired eyes.

You know my friends call me *Sleepy* and that I live up to the name not only by night, but often by day as well. I wish I could share some of this experience with you. The Bible sees sleep as a gift, or suggests that the Lord pours out gifts on his beloved while she slumbers. (Psalm 127)

Sleep is indeed a blessing enabling us to cease from anxious toil and to surrender to the arms of the one who himself rested on the seventh day. The dark veil of night covers us from the glare and the glamour that would keep our eyes from closing.

The French writer Peguy used the image of sleep to show how this sweet surrender into the hands of Divine Providence could be accomplished. He puts the following words into the mouth of God: 'It has come to my ears that there are men who do not sleep. I cannot abide people who do not sleep. Sleep is, perhaps, the most glorious thing in my creation. I myself rested on the seventh day.'

Sleep presupposes night and the self-surrender of sleep is, or should be, our constant, uninterrupted attitude. Night is the all-enveloping ocean that embraces the islands of our days. We think that the day is important. We have the ability to work, but do not have the virtue of being able to do nothing, to relax, to rest, to sleep. We conduct our affairs very well during the day. But we will not let God look after them at night.'

Peguy goes on to tell of how on one particular night, God came down like a linen cloth to cover the body of his dead Son. It shrouded his sleep in ultimate self-surrender to the Father.

I once came across the half joke, half-earnest remark: *No one should work who has the strength to lie in bed*. It may be no harm to realise that the world will get on all right when we are gone. We have to stop acting like God and trying to manage the unmanageable. We may have to learn how to live with the agony of ambiguity and with the ragged edges of life.

Which reminds me, beloved, of something I observed in Stephen's Green pond, where the ducks make their home. The creatures make a splendid sight in their vivid colours and their avid playfulness. The city office workers often share bits of their lunches with them, and children off from school find the ducks and their antics to be sheer magic. But this day, along came Smart Alec who tried to fish one of the ducks out and take him home. He thought he could manage to tame the wild and wondrous creature in his own back garden.

That's the way it sometimes is with ourselves. We think we can deal our own hand, manage things our own way, make others fit into our little scheme, manipulate and control them. We forget that God has a plan and a purpose for each one of us. We try to keep our flying ducks in a row, or fit them in to a pattern not of God's making.

'Behold the birds of the air,' said Jesus. 'Your heavenly Father feeds them. So stop worrying and go to sleep. You'll be all right.' We just have to let God feed the birds and deal with the ducks as he sees fit. Our little ways are not always his ways. We have to learn to let others be, especially at night when it is time to shut our eyes.

Beloved, as you turn in for sleep, commend yourself and all your cares to the Lord with the assurance of these words:

> I will bless the Lord, who gives me counsel,
> Who even at night directs my heart.
> I keep the Lord ever in my sight,
> Since he is at my right hand, I shall stand firm.
> And so my heart rejoices, my soul is glad,
> Even my body shall rest in safety.
> (Psalm 15)

Enthusiasm

Beloved,

A love such as ours is a walk in faith, an adventure in grace. We can be tempted to play safe, to take no risks. Courage may fail. We may refuse to run the race without counting the cost. What if we are misunderstood and are condemned to a fate worse than death. We still have to get out of the boat and venture on the stormy sea. Will we sink and be lost?

There is an example of this courage in the story of Captain Pat Etheridge of the US Coast Guard. One night in the howling hurricane, the lookout saw a distress signal from a ship that had gone aground on the dangerous Diamond Shoals, ten miles to sea. The lifeboats were ordered out. One of the life guards protested, 'Captain Pat, we can get out there, but we can never get back.' 'Boys,' came the reply that has gone down in history, 'we don't have to come back.'

Jesus gave his life for the love that was in his heart. He has commanded that the gospel be preached in all the world. He has not promised his friends an easy time. He has not given the assurance of a safe return to the homebase – but he did say 'Go!'

> Who answers God's insistent call,
> Must give himself, his life, his all,
> His purposes are unshaken.
> Who sets his hand unto the plough
> and glances back with anxious brow,
> His calling hath mistaken.

Our mission is to be a living flame of love, a flame that will light up the sea on which we sail. We have to be, not casual workers, but dedicated enthusiasts who carry the fire of divine love in our bosoms.

All great movements have come from those who have enkindled fires, where others might have sat on in the cold and darkness. The word enthusiasm is derived from two Greek words: *en* meaning in, and *theos* meaning God. Enthusiasm is literally God in us. The enthusiastic person is one who speaks as if he or she were possessed by God.

This quality is the most important factor in selling goods and getting things done. One of the largest advertisers of any single product came to Chicago with less than fifty dollars in his pocket. Wrigley now sells many millions of dollars worth of his chewing gum every year, and on the wall of his private office hang the framed words of Emerson: *Nothing great was ever achieved without enthusiasm.*

Beloved, this is the question we must ask: Are we enthusiastic for the highest calling of all, the kingdom of Jesus Christ? Our constant prayer is that we may run this race together in his love.

Be still

Beloved,

I have already written to you about sleep and about resting in the arms of Jesus. A spirit of stillness and rest should pervade our whole life.

In case you think I'm running away from you, let me assure you that I do not need to go alone into the forest to find stillness, nor do I have to take a formal holiday out to find rest. I find this rest when we are together in peace, especially when we are in the presence of the Blessed Sacrament of the Eucharist. I like to whisper those words of Psalm 66: *O God, be gracious and bless us and let your face shine upon us.*

My temptation is to keep myself busy and occupied. They say that the busy mind is a troubled mind, the quiet mind is a wholesome mind, but the still mind is a divine mind.

Jesus said, 'Martha you are troubled about many things but only one is needed.' A troubled mind keeps us awake at night and disturbs us through the day.

We long for peace of mind. We are surrounded by noise that wrecks not only our peace but can damage our physical well-being into the bargain. I pity those whose ears are continually bombarded by strident sound and blatant music. We long for an oasis of quiet and inner stillness. We seek that silent blessing which falls like the dew of heaven upon the ground of our being.

The gospel tells of certain people who were so busy that they could not accept their invitation to the wedding feast. They said 'No' to God himself. They were troubled in mind even if they may not have realised it.

We all get hassled from life when we allow ourselves to become preoccupied with it. We have to learn to live well in both worlds, working our way through the daily ground beneath us, without losing sight of the heaven above us.

It is not just the hurly-burly of the market place that disturbs us. The privacy of home and the core of our being is invaded by this pollution of noise and agitation. Violence on the telly, and the blare of hi-fi units keep up a sustained attack on the tranquillity we so often long for. Drink, drugs and addiction to nicotine add to the problem.

Double-glazed windows may keep out the noise from the street. But one can't be shielded from the noise that rumbles within. Stillness, which is of the divine mind, goes beyond mere quiet or external silence. Inner stillness can overcome the noise from outside. It is born of that peace, which Jesus spoke of before leaving this troubled world. 'My peace I leave with you, not as the world gives do I give to you.'

Jesus himself is our peace. He invites us to be still like Mary, who has chosen the better part. He leads us by quiet waters to the inner cave of silence and stillness. Gabrielle Bossis heard Jesus speak to her after Holy Communion: *Enjoy me. Give yourself a rest from saying prayers, so that you may enjoy my love.*

There is a hunger these times for the prayer of stillness. Traditionally, this has been known as contemplation, though many today call it meditation. There are many teachers of this way of prayer. We have books that tell of interior silence and of the inner eye of love. Those who teach meditation use what they call a mantra, a word or sound that is repeated over and over again to the rhythm of one's breathing. Christians tend to use a sacred word like Alleluia or Come Lord Jesus.

Instead of causing fatigue or monotony, the rhythmic repetition brings stillness to the troubled mind. The rhythm of the Hail Mary in the Rosary, repeated on the beads, is meant to have this same effect. While Eastern mantras are man-made and often associated with some pagan deity, the sacred sounds of the Our Father and the Hail Mary are heaven-sent. The still mind of those who pray the Rosary in a lingering love with Jesus, is indeed a participation in the divine mind.

Beloved, I know how hard you try to say the Rosary. There may, however, be times when you should simply pause to enjoy the Lord. St Catherine of Siena did just that, when she became a little weary saying the form of Rosary that was common in her day.

The Healing Sound

Beloved,

The church was full one night, but the organist's seat was empty. I'm a great believer in the healing power of music and of song to bring healing to soul and body. So it was a bit of an up-hill battle struggling with just my own poor words.

As I looked out on the many sick and troubled people before me, I thought of the shepherd David, who would play music and sing to King Saul. In a fit of anger, Saul once flung a weapon at the singer. But the effect of David's music was to bring ease of mind and heart to the worried Saul.

Before the healing service had begun, a lady had come to me to pour out her tale of woe. As it was, I couldn't do much for her, as time was moving in on us. So I told her to come back to see me on another occasion.

In the middle of the sermon, I noticed a young man who was an organist in another church, walk in at the back. His trained eye and his well-tuned ear must have observed that there was no one in command of the music situation. So what do you think he did? He walked right up to the organ and took his seat. At the Offertery, he launched into Sibellius' *Findlandia*. The splendour of the haunting music touched me so deeply, I cannot find words to describe it. But what I still recall was the hush that came over the congregation.

I asked the altar server to tell the organist to repeat the piece during the distribution of Holy Communion. When all was over, the lady who had come to me before we began, marched surely and sweetly up the centre aisle and said, 'Father, I'm all right now. That music brought me the peace and healing that I needed.'

I know, beloved, that you are familiar with the music, but you may not have the words that have been attached as a hymn to that splendid air. I find them precious and I frequently repeat them to myself and use them at Masses for divine healing. I wish to share them with you, that you too may speak them.

Be still my soul, the Lord is on your side.
Leave to your God to order and provide.
In every change, he faithful will remain.
Be still my soul.

Your God will undertake to guide the future
As he has the past.
Be still my soul.
The tempests still obey his voice
Who ruled them once in Galilee.

If you are still struggling, beloved, with getting to sleep, I recommend that you keep the above lines beside your bed and read them as part of your night prayer. By the way, you know that I talk and write too much. My mother told me that if I could sing, nothing would stop me. Perhaps it is as well that I am mainly on the receiving end of music and song, but I assure you that it is a good place to be.

The Long Walk

Beloved,

You sent me such a wonderful *Thank you* letter, that I have kept it on my desk to read over and over again. But what I want to let you know is that doing little services for you is never a chore, never a burden. Where there is love there is no labour. Between ourselves, I just might be a little jealous if another stepped in to take over the task. It is a delight to be on your majesty's service!

You mention the long journey I made in the cold and the rain. Now I wouldn't want it to be a case of *I'd go through fire and water for you and I'll see you tonight as long as it isn't raining!* Making the journey is a kind of pilgrimage and I savour the whole experience, from leaving home to getting to your place.

Did you hear of the young African pupil who brought a gift to the teacher? It was a stunningly beautiful shell, found only on a remote island beach. The teacher was deeply moved and realised that the girl must have walked many miles to find the shell. 'You shouldn't have gone to so much trouble to find such a gift.' she said. Wise beyond her tender years, the child replied: 'The long walk is part of the gift.' It reminds one of the statements made by St Catherine of Siena: 'All the way to heaven, is heaven too.'

Gifts begin in the heart. Before they are picked up in the hand or given over to another, they are conceived in the heart. The love and service that we lavish on each other, come from wellsprings that lie deep within the human spirit. They often derive from our long walk with each other. Christ's gift too, began with a long journey from the high hills of heaven into the valleys of earth. His healing gifts were poured out on broken humanity as he climbed the hills of Jerusalem and walked the dusty roads of Galilee and struggled painfully to Calvary.

Beloved, you are my companion on life's walk, and we must remember this story next time we pray the Sorrowful mysteries of the Rosary together. They are our long walk of love with Jesus.

The tree of the Cross is
our song, our strength and our salvation.
As we meet it on the long walk of life,
may it bring us the gift of new life.

We lift our hearts to bless you.
We hold out our hands
to receive all that you wish to pour out upon us.

The valley of darkness and depression

Beloved,

You and I have been asking that the Lord would use our love as a life-source for others. The prayer I often make before the Blessed Sacrament, is:

Lord Jesus, make us an instrument of your healing love.

In our shared ministry, isn't it those who suffer from depression and darkness that seem mostly to come our way? I continue to be amazed at the number of brilliant, intelligent people who become victims of this illness. While we appreciate the wonder of doctors and drugs, we need to keep turning towards the divine light that illuminates our darkness.

Depression in one or other of its forms, touches all ages, even young adults. They complain of not feeling well, of loss of energy and enthusiasm. They experience physical pain and exhaustion for no apparent reason. They experience loneliness and imagine life has lost all meaning, sometimes thinking they are going mad. Yet it can be a fruitful creative period, a deeply spiritual experience, a dark night such as the mystics speak of.

Life is seldom without shadow, and some of the soul's power comes from its shadow qualities. Many of the world's great minds have produced work of wondrous beauty during these dark periods. Vincent Van Gogh painted his masterpiece *Sunflowers* while in the depths of depression.

What brings on this dark terror? Loss of work, and of personal esteem? Heartache over broken relationships?

Continuous and instant stimulation, loud blatant music, excessive smoking, noise-pollution, alcohol and other drugs which bring on exaggerated highs, all contribute. Normal low-key living becomes difficult to achieve. Living on a high for too long, and knowing little of stillness and silence, can bring about a dive into the dark valley of depression. At the same time, there are many good and deeply religious persons who live quiet gentle lives, but who fall victim to this illness without any apparent reason.

Thomas Moore, who was a monk for twelve years and has degrees in theology, music and philosophy, offers a positive approach which is helpful. He sees depression as part of life's spiritual journey. 'We are afraid,' he says, 'of the spiritual space the soul so desperately needs for survival. We fill it with television running, when no one is watching, or with a radio playing all day long, as a defence against silence. For the ancients, the states of sadness and melancholy, far from being something negative and soul-destroying, provided a rite of passage and purification through the darkness into ultimate life and hope.'

He says that in olden times people kept a bower dedicated to the Deity, a dark shaded place where one could retire, without fear of being disturbed. Sometimes people need to withdraw.

The family or community should be the normal refuge from the frenzy of pressure. That is where we should learn the wholesome unity of body, mind and spirit. We need havens of peace where we can be in touch with the stillness of God. Family prayer should not be an optional extra, but a vital ingredient in the maintenance of wholeness. It is a preventive medicine which does more good than all the counselling and medication in the world.

Depression is usually presented as a hopeless condition with nothing to hold on to, a feeling that nobody understands and nobody cares. Maybe, we have at times to accept this situation. Life is a mystery and may not seem logical to our puny minds. But life is larger than logic. Often when all doors seem closed, God opens a window of light.

Let us pray, beloved, that we may be able to filter something of this light of faith to those who come our way. I am always impressed by the manner in which you listen in love, to those we meet on our walk through town. I think of the young men who were sitting drinking in the rain. I wanted to walk on, but you stood still. Your smile must have been a light to them as they sat in the the shadows and on the margins of life. I want to share with you a prayer which I wrote some years ago:

Dear Jesus, I walk in the valley of darkness, for I suffer from depression. I feel unloved, rejected, useless to myself and useless to others. I feel lost in a world I no longer understand. At times, I want to sleep and never wake up again. Lord, I believe that your love is a transforming love. Jesus, Son of David, have pity on me. Out of the depths I cry to you.

Lord, even though I feel nothing, I still praise you for the wonder of my being. You have formed me in my mother's womb, and watched over me to this moment. I am precious in your eyes and you love me. On the cross, you shed your blood for me. You have carved me on the palm of your hand. For all this I give you thanks and praise.

May your precious blood give new life to me and to all those who suffer as I do. Take each one of us and hug us to your sacred and loving heart. Through your glorious wounds may we be healed.

Dear Jesus, when you fed the crowd in the desert, you wished to gather up the fragments lest anything be lost. As I wander through a desert and darkness of my own, I ask you to gather up the fragments of this shattered being lest anything be lost. Through the prophet Joel you promised to restore the years that the locusts have eaten. I ask you, lay your hands gently on my weary head and restore me. Let your face shine upon me and give me back the peace and the joy that has forsaken me.

Beloved, you know how weak we are when trying to help others through this valley of darkness. So let's pray as I have started this letter, hoping that the good Lord will make us a united instrument of his healing love.

Only a tin box on wheels!

Beloved,

You know how upset I was over the lady who went off with the office car and never came back. As the song has it, *The lady is a tramp!* We have not had sight of her, or the car, for three weeks. You can imagine how I have tossed on the bed at night, waiting and wondering and preparing the words to dole out if ever she did show up! I've gone so far as to half hope she would come to a sticky end as she drives round in our brand new Nissan Micra.

Frustration and anger and bitterness have been eating into my soul and making my body distinctly uncomfortable. Prayer had become one terrible distraction, no tribute to God and no help to myself.

Then, beloved, you met me as I was pacing up and down the drive like a demented animal. You listened in love as you always did and said, 'Let her have it and wish her well. After all it's only a bit of tin on wheels!'

You remember how shocked I was at your suggestion. My lovely shining red chariot, my lovely Nissan Micra! And then to let this Lady Tramp off the hook!

'That's like the sermon on the Mount,' I replied. 'You can't surely mean to let her hit me on the other cheek and walk away Scott free.'

'Exactly,' you calmly answered. 'Isn't that the gospel you are supposed to be preaching? If they ask for your cloak, give them your shirt as well. Think no more about it. Let your prisoner free and you'll be free yourself.'

Crazy! My first reaction was as if I had been hit by a stun gun. You sure stopped me in my tracks. But because you are a woman of such belief in the gospel and because you spoke only in love, I soon fell into line.

So here I am, beloved, writing to tell you that this whole messy affair has turned out to be one of the greatest blessings I have experienced in life. I have taken the gospel message you put before me with complete trust and have never regretted it. You may not have the vocation to stand in the pulpit every Sunday and deliver a sermon, but you are a true evangelist and a preacher in your own spirit-filled fashion.

I should add a PS to this, saying that while one car went off on its own, I was never lacking a set of wheels under me to wander from one end of the country to the other. Maybe too, as I let the lady and the car tramp their merry way, the Lord will have mercy on me for all my own devious and doubtful deals.

You see, beloved, that while I write to you at times in strong terms, I am weak and have a lot to learn. So keep on preaching the gospel of love and mercy to me.

Let the river run

Beloved,

There are times when I am tempted to give up. I seem to be going round in circles and getting no where.

You comfort me with the assuring words of your last letter: *All you need is to be light enough to float, and just heavy enough to hold together.*

You quote Barry Stevens who told his folk:

'Don't push the river. It flows by itself! Things could be easier, if only we could let ourselves float gently along the river of life. We worry about our family and friends, our health, our job, our finances. We get hurt on the surface and in the shallows. But deep down inside, the river of life runs on. All we need is to be light enough to float, and just heavy enough to hold together.

If only we could realise that the surface and the edges are of lesser importance. It is the deep down centre that matters. There at the inner core of the being, Christ lives and reigns and has his seat of government. We need only to relax and let him be in control.'

You have reminded me of the time I was staying a few weeks in the country, and would be wakened each morning with the farmer singing at the top of his voice: *Reign, Master Jesus, reign!* Like every farmer he had worries about milk quotas and falling prices for beef, but I never saw him cast down. He smiled his way round the farm and called every cow and bullock by a pet name.

Worry does not solve anything. In any case it is downright disobedience to a solemn commandment: 'Do not worry about your life, what you will eat or what you will drink ...' Of course, we have to look in some measure to the future. We have to make plans, but when we have made all the provision we can, we must leave something to the angels.

Perhaps the secret is to learn how to savour the present moment, to live fully alive to the present situation, and totally present to the person before me. It is amazing how certain great personalities with heavy timetables know how to give you their total attention and treat you as if you were the only one in their lives. When they are with you, they are not looking over the shoulder to see who is next in line. The trouble with so many of us is that we race ahead of ourselves and of those around us. Fretful about the future and worried about the past, we lose out on the present. Our God is a God of now.

Helen Mallicoat puts it well in her poem, *I am:*

> I was regretting the past and fearing the future.
> Suddenly my Lord was speaking:
> My name is I am
> When you live in the past with its mistakes and regrets
> It is hard, I am not there.
> My name is not I was
> When you live in the future with its problems and fears
> It is hard, I am not there.
> My name is not I will be
> When you live in this moment, it is not hard,
> My name is I am

Give the stars away!

Beloved,

When I was in Lourdes, I was given a present of a beautiful and precious rosary beads. I kept them in a fine purse and loved to look at them and feel them between my fingers as I prayed. When they were blessed with holy water and prayed over by the priest who had entrusted them to me, I experienced a certain closeness to Jesus in his sacred mysteries. They were indeed not only something to hold on to, but someone to cling to.

Then one day, during a train journey, as I was praying on them, I met up with a young man who told me his horrific life-story as he offered me a drink from the store of liquor he had in his case. When he came to the end of his story, I said, 'John, you've told it all, even your sins. That's as good a confession as ever you'll make, so I may as well give you forgiveness and ask for the loving mercy of Jesus on your life.' He asked me to write to his mother and say, 'Mum I love you and want you to know, your prayers have been answered. I've made my confession and am going the right road from now on.'

As I promised to do so, something inside me said, 'You may never see this guy again. You must leave him some reminder of this graced moment.' As I whispered the words to myself, I looked down at the precious rosary beads still in my hands. Could I part with them?

Before I could answer, I was blurting out, 'John, I want you to have this beads as a bond between us.'

'I can't,' he said, 'they are too beautiful, too precious for you to give them away.'

'That's why I want you to have them. I wouldn't give you trash. Keep them and use them and not only will your Mum be happy, but your Mother in heaven will smile on you.'

That was the last I saw of John. Soon after, I got a telephone message from his Mum. She said that John had been killed in an accident. Between her tears, she said, 'the undertaker found a beautiful rosary beads in his pocket and brought it to me. I would never have understood, only that I got your letter saying that John had asked you to write saying how he loved me.'

Beloved, you and I have a love of simplicity and poverty. We try to practice detachment from the goods of this world. But well we know that as we give away, we are given back a hundred-fold. You may have heard about the Zen monk who knew this secret only too well.

He was very poor and lived alone in the forest. One night as he lay asleep a burglar broke in to his small hut. Knowing that there was nothing much to take, he said to the thief, 'I have only the clothes I worked in today, but take them, I don't need them now that I'm in bed. I've all I want for the moment.' Totally surprised, the thief grabbed the clothes and started to run out the the door.

'Wait,' said the monk, 'there's something more I want to give you. Take this precious stone. It is all that's left of my family fortune.'

Did the monk have any regrets? No. He sat there looking at the beauty of the night and said, sadly, 'I wish he would have stayed around a little longer. I could have given him the stars.'

Months later, the monk was walking in the forest, when who comes on the scene but the very same thief. This time things turned out differently.

'I've brought you back your treasure' said the thief. 'Keep your precious stone, but give me your secret – the hidden power, the grace that enabled you to part with everything.'

Beloved, there is a hidden power, a secret, that enables us to rise above the world of physical and material things, even the precious stones of earth, and sea and sky. You and I must dare to give the stars away.

Despite the Scandals

Beloved,

You know only too well the depression that settles on so many these days as they read of the various scandals in the church. For a celibate clergy, it is doubly painful. Many have lived up to their sacred vows, and perhaps struggled with the temptations and trials. In recent years, there has been a serious effort to form young men and women in the whole area of sexuality and relationships.

My own experience was not so good and I find that many of my contemporaries see celibacy as a burden that makes life extremely difficult. They feel lonely, unloved and unappreciated. Without being consciously aware of it, they desperately need someone to say to them, 'You are loveable.' Or indeed to look them in the eyes, and say straight out, 'I love you.'

I am comforted by your remark, that 'despite the upheavals, scandals and distresses in the church, the great river of divine love flows on. Underlying the structures and the personnel and the newspaper headlines, this river of life has flowed on without interruption for two thousand years. It will continue to flow as the Spirit moves the hearts of God's people.'

Whatever our perception of the church may be, it is still the bride of Christ and we love it and know that, individually, we are enfolded in its love. Every Christian call, whether to action, to speech, to suffering or to prayer, is ultimately a call to love. The saints agree that love is the centre of the Christian church. St Teresa of the Child Jesus became a saint through grasping this truth. Observing the many ministries operating among the people of God, she realised that 'love was the true motive-force which enabled the members of the church to act. If love ceased to function, the apostles would forget to preach, the martyrs would refuse to shed their blood. Love is the vocation which includes all others. It is a universe of its own, encompassing time and space. It is eternal. I discovered where it is that I belong in the church, to be nothing else than love, deep down in the heart of mother church.'

Love is a gift from God and must be sought through fidelity to prayer and by diligent searching of the scriptures. As we leave ourselves open to the drive of the Spirit, this love leads to divine ecstasy and to spiritual marriage with God. Whoever is united with God becomes one spirit with him. Divine love flows into human living, making for ease and sweetness, often solving hitherto insurmountable problems. Where this spirit reigns, there is neither violence nor harshness.

An attraction for God on our part, is a sign of his even greater attraction for us. When these two attractions fuse together we are on the high road to union with God. We have joined the great and eternal river of contemplative life and love. We find the beauty ever ancient, ever new, as St Augustine described it. The hail and the storm, the wind and the rain may buffet the external structure of the church, but the soul that has learned to linger in love with the Lord has nothing to fear.

Do not judge

Beloved,

It is one of the occupational hazards of those in public life that they have at times to cast a critical eye over others and make decisions on difficult situations that arise in the course of their work.

The folly of snap judgements of others is well illustrated by the story of the late Bishop Potter of New York. He was sailing for Europe in one of the great transatlantic liners. When he went on board, he found another passenger was to share the cabin with him. After going to see his accommodation, he came up to the purser's desk and inquired if he could leave his gold watch and other valuables in the ship's safe. He explained that ordinarily he never availed himself of that privilege, but he had been to his cabin and had met the man who was to occupy the other berth and, judging from his appearance, was afraid that he might not be a very trustworthy person. The purser accepted the responsibility of caring for the valuables and remarked, 'It's all right, Bishop, I'll be very glad to take care of them for you. The other man has been up here and left his for the same reason.'

Instead of making snap judgements, beloved, we ought to pray for the gift of counsel to enable us to be patient and prudent in our decisions.

Good Counsel and fraternal correction

Beloved,

I often say that you know my own mind better than myself. Maybe it is your heart that lets you know what I should really be thinking and doing. You are not only the wind beneath my wings. You give me a kick-start when I'm dithering and doubting. Strange thing, too, is that I do not resent your sisterly correction. Were it not for you, I would not change my clothes often enough or even take a shower when needed. I smile when I think how you told me that I was not presentable to God or man the way I kept my hair. I try to remember how you told me to walk out on the altar with dignity, not to waddle out like a sick sailor on deck, but to hold my back straight and my head erect.

I'm like the Chief Constable of Manchester who has been described as God's own policeman. He freely admitted that he had made many mistakes. However, looking back on thirty five years with a superb police force he remarked: 'My best counsellor was my own wife. Despite all my studies and experience I was often baffled. It was my wife who was my best assistant. She gave me advice and pulled me out of many tight corners. She had a kind of insight – a sixth sense.'

Wisdom looks out on the wide panorama of life so as to advance our knowledge. Counsel is that sixth sense that gets down to fine detail and enables us to make decisions in particular situations. There is a basic human gift of counsel that runs through every human lifestyle, but those who allow God to take over, experience counsel as a special gift of the Holy Spirit.

The best practical judgement, left to its own devices, finds itself baffled in the midst of individual incidents. It has to be lifted up and instructed by God who comprehends everything, even the finest detail. Here is where the Holy Spirit's gift of counsel comes in. By it, people come sweetly and surely to decisions, beyond their own prudential resources. We operate no longer out of our own meagre resources, but live securely out of the infinite supply of God.

Beloved, you share something of the swiftness and clarity with which Our Lady observed the situation at the marriage feast of Cana. She observed the moment to moment developments among the guests and the waiters. She anticipated the embarrassment which would have ensued had there been no wine for the rest of the celebration. She knew exactly when to intervene, and when to intercede with her Son.

Beloved, you are the lady who accompanies me to the wedding feast of life. I can never tell you how much I rely on your inspired gift of counsel.

Love Rachel

Beloved,

My heart went out to you when I read your letter about Rachel. I know how much you love her, and how sad you feel at the thought of Rachel and all her family praying for Messiah to come. You are filled, you say, with a burning desire to try to convince her that Messiah has indeed come, and is living among us. Well, you are not the first Christian to feel like that, beloved!

I remember having a conversation many years ago with a very dear Dominican brother of mine, who had spent many years in Tehran. He was similarly filled with a desire to convert all of Islam to Christianity. When he first arrived in Iran, he told me, he spent many long nights in fervent conversation with Muslim friends, trying to convert them. The best response he ever got was: 'Well, if you're so great, why aren't you a Muslim too?'

My feeling is that there are some things we must leave to the Holy Spirit! During all of his lifetime on earth, Jesus gave his disciples only one new commandment: *You must love your neighbour as yourself.* He told them they must love even their enemies. And that is the great gift he has given to all baptised Christians – the gift of love. We who know the Lord, and know that he is living within us, must learn to radiate his love into the very air around us. He doesn't ask anything else of us.

You know that in the past some terrible mistakes were made in this area. Great Christian armies went off to wage war against Judaism and Islam, but we are living now in wonderful times when the Holy Spirit is working mightily throughout the whole world, bringing peace and reconciliation where there was hatred and war in former centuries. Peacemaking is not easy, but if we could only learn to love one another, as Jesus told us, what a wonderful world this would be! We must learn to respect the religious beliefs of other people, while nourishing our own faith in prayer and utter trust in the Lord, who died to save us from hatred and fear. With regard to Rachel, then, the best thing you can do is just continue to love her, and hope that she might see something of Jesus in you. Remember, St Paul told you that you are the temple of the Holy Spirit. The sanctuary lamp is burning in your heart and anyone who loves you will come to see that in time. We must leave it to God to sort out the differences between Christians and Jews and Moslems; only he can accomplish such mighty work.

If all Christians were what a Christian was supposed to be, the whole world would be converted in a generation. Our task is to love everybody, to praise God, and to pray that we will not interfere in his glorious plan for the whole of creation. The prayer of *The Lady of all Nations*, asking Jesus to send the Holy Spirit among us, can bring about the fulfilment of all God's promises to his people:

> Lord Jesus Christ, Son of the Father,
> send now your Spirit over the earth.
> Let the Holy Spirit live in the hearts of all nations,
> that they may be preserved
> from degeneration, disaster and war.
> May the Lady of all Nations, who once was Mary,
> be our Advocate. Amen.

Abide with me

Beloved,

The official Night Prayer of the church contains the lovely old hymn *Abide with me*. I like to rest in that simple word, *abide*. It reminds me of Jesus, when he promised that those who loved him would experience this home-making in the heart. 'If anyone loves me, my Father will love him and we will come and make our abode with him.'

The tale is told of a young soldier who lay mortally wounded on the battle-ield facing the evening of his life. The commanding officer told the dying man the story of Jesus who stayed to rest with the disciples on the road to Emmaus: *Abide with us, for it is toward evening and the day is far spent.*

The strained, worried look vanished from the dying soldier's face, replaced by a peaceful, almost happy expression. Then he whispered, 'Thank you for telling me that story, Sir. *Abide with me* is my mother's favourite hymn. I shall be able to sleep now.'

There are times, beloved, when worry takes over our night's repose. In the darkness of night, that hymn can have a soothing calm. I wouldn't mind someone singing it at the evening of my own life:

> Abide with me, fast falls the eventide,
> The darkness deepens, Lord, with me abide,
> When other helpers fail, and comforts flee,
> Help of the helpless!
> O abide with me.
> Swift to its close ebbs out life's little day,
> Earth's joys grow dim, its glories pass away.
> Change and decay in all around I see,
> O thou who changest not, abide with me.
>
> Hold thou thy Cross before my closing eyes,
> Shine through the gloom, and point me to the skies.
> Heaven's morning breaks, and earth's vain shadows flee,
> In life, in death, O Lord, abide with me.

Henry Francis Lyte was a dying man himself when he wrote this hymn, and he knew it. The words *fast falls the eventide* refer not just to the close of day, but to the evening of life.

For 25 years Lyte had been vicar of the Devonshire fishing village of Brixham. At the age of 54 his health had broken and he was preparing to leave for the south of France. His consoling hymn was written shortly before his departure. He died at Nice a few weeks later of consumption. Not surprisingly then, his hymn foreshadows death. But still more, it is a hymn about faith, the sort of faith that faces every circumstance with trust in the power of the cross and in the unfailing mercy of God.

Beloved, as you and I let the Lord abide in us, we come to abide more and more in each other. I pray that Jesus living in us, may lead us through the darkness to unending light. Someone has written: *Death will come and take my love away.* May our love be so refined in the furnace of divine love, that it may never be taken away.

Come Sister Death

Beloved,

You already know my thoughts about death. I don't want to take it lying down in the sense of it being a defeat, the end as it were of life and love and all that is good. I want to go out with a cry of delight and victory. But some have faulted me for this seeming arrogance, saying that I was dictating terms to God. One such objector wrote:

> 'I am an ex-nurse and have seen death at close quarters, in war and peace. Believe me, there is nothing very joyful in actually dying. You will be disillusioned if you think that when you are gasping your last breath, it will be beautiful, and that you will be happy with relations or neighbours all around you. Jesus was not being very happy when he cried out, *Why have you forsaken me?* He felt so alone, his spirit bereft of comfort. His mother saw it and wept for him. Nearly all my patients have cried out to me: 'Nurse, please can I have a drink of water?' I think of Jesus crying: 'I thirst.' They only gave him vinegar to drink.
>
> I hope there will be someone to hold your hand and comfort you, dear Father, when you are dying. There are many who die without a single soul to help them. I myself do not feel as you do, that it is a time for celebration. You may not even know of the time when the Lord will call you, but I should warn you that there may not be time to notify your loved ones to come around your bed! As for the statement about going out in a blaze of glory ... fireworks, a band playing loud music ... God forbid, Father Gabriel. You will not be launching a ship!'

There you are, beloved. Clearly others do not see things as I do. The point I was trying to make, is that I wish my death to be something positive, the supreme sacrifice of life. I believe that it is never too early to place ourselves in the hands of God, saying,

Into your hands I commend my spirit. When death came for Jesus, he cried in a loud voice, *It is finished!* That was not a cry of despair. It was the confirmation of his victory. It was the statement that the battle was over, that the enemy was routed and the work was finished, accomplished!

I just want to make sure that my death is in that same spirit, a sacrificial and joyful offering rather than a destructive end. What I may have to suffer, or what my reactions may be, I know not. I may indeed be wracked with pain and scarcely able to cope. When the hour comes, I would like you, beloved, to pray that I may be brave and say,

> *Here I come Lord, sealed in the blood of your covenant.*
> *I do not ask for justice, I trust in your merciful love.*

St Francis of Assisi said, *Welcome, Sister Death!*

Beloved, I urge you to hold on to this glorious promise: If the Spirit of him who raised Jesus from the dead, dwells in you, he who raised Christ Jesus from the dead, will give life to your mortal bodies also, through his Spirit who dwells in you. (Romans 8:12)

In this life, we are like unborn children in gestation. Death is our birth to eternal life and that's why we speak of the death of the saints, as their birthday. May your death be a happy birthday, beloved!

Because you have helped me through life, I would dearly love to have you near when death is nigh, as indeed I would wish to be near to you in your hour of need. Being part of an all male religious community, however, that is unlikely. This helps to instil into our souls the truth that however close we may be, our personal vocation and our obedience to God's providence governs all our ways.

Edmond Holmes describes death as the eternal love dawning on our inner eyes:

> Stronger than life is death, for death subdues
> Life's flaring torchlight with its argent rays.
> Stronger than death is life, for life renews
> Through death the firesprings of its vanished days.

Stronger than death is love, for love through death
Kindles a larger life when life expires.
Life – what is life? Love's foreglow in the skies.
Death – what is death? Love dawning on our eyes.

'I will divinise natural love'

Beloved,

There is a price to be paid for climbing into God's love and I believe that you are ready to pay it. Jesus is most willing to help us acquire this pearl of great price.

I would like to share with you something ofwhat the Lord has been saying to me:

'I will pour out my love, the love of my heart through my wounds, upon all those who give me their loving attention in the sacrament of my love. Through this love, wounds will he healed, wounds of the mind and heart and soul, wounds that impair the flow of human, natural love between persons. I will divinise natural love between persons who seek to love through my Divine Humanity.

All those willing to love within the Divine Humanity, will find my heart a ready refuge in their perplexities. They shall be shielded therein from the harsh misconstructions of others.

The enjoyment of human love is my dispensation. Those who seek to love beyond, without or far from me, may for a time enjoy a purely physical sensation which, when shriven of its initial attractions, leaves an emptiness and even bitterness, which leave their souls far from me. If am sought, through human loving, if I am understood and accepted, as the Author, the Giver, the Source of love, then my support, my tendemess and my power will give to those who love, an understanding of the true meaning of love and the true beginning and end of human life on earth. I will enter into your flesh and chasten it and I will make it sweet to love.'

In His time

Beloved,

You tell me that you have little time left to accomplish the mission the Lord has entrusted to you. You speak about work – about getting this and that done.

You must enter the inner land to discover the core of your being. God will then act and fruit will appear. Often we spoil what God is going to give us, by grasping and trying to possess in advance what he plans to give us sweetly in his own time.

You can't go quicker than God's pace. There are those who won't wait. They think they can take shortcuts. The loving willingness to go at his pace is what counts.

You must leave the norms of the world behind. You might achieve in ten seconds what you have striven after for a whole lifetime, but in another way – when it is God's moment.

As God enters through the spirit, he enters also into the body. But until we have joined him willingly where he is, in our land, there will be pain. But what he promised, the joy that no man shall take from us, is at the end of that pain, that journey. When the soul has grasped this, it will never falter until it reaches that point where true freedom is, and all its expressions.

Unified in God, the whole being comes alive, really alive. We are ready to enter the kingdom of God from which nothing is missing, even in this world. It is because they do not realise this, that celibates fail to understand that they are called to the enjoyment of deep love. Celibates are called specially to love. You are meant to enjoy love. There is no enjoyment outside God.

The rhythm of God is beating through all humanity and all must be given up to God. In his time he is going to sweep into you and right through you. This will in no way rob you of your humanity, but simply transform it, so that it shares in his divinity. This is the result of the death and resurrection of Jesus.

This way of loving, is straight, but the terrain is broad. If you let God's rhythm beat out to the last, it will end in a symphony.

We must never exclude Jesus, the Divine Humanity, in whom all things hold together. He has obtained this gift for us that we may integrate it securely and happily with the total flow of our own divinised personality.

Jesus says: 'Beware of negative teachings alone in regard to your sexuality; for consecrated to me, I will preserve you, to balance and develop this integral part of being. Likewise does Satan seek to play upon the wounds which we have sustained in this area.'

Healing comes through his wounds

Beloved,

I know that you have suffered much in recent times, but I want to assure you that through your wounds pressed to the glorious wounds of Jesus, you will bring great healing to many others. God does not wish suffering for its own sake. It is simply that he wishes to work his marvels for you, where he dwells within. In this way you come to sing your own Magnificat – to glory in the mighty deeds the Lord is doing in your own life. God does not want to cut away anything of your true personality – he wants to refine you and prepare you for great happenings.

In order that these happenings may be completely yours – intrinsically yours – you may have to suffer. This is to establish you out of the mass of humanity, and make you a true individual autonomous personality. Thus, you are built up into a mature person, and God is able to develop you into your full potential, in the place where he dwells.

This is why it is necessary to go apart and allow the sword to enter. Those who do not accept the sword involve themselves in all kinds of distractions and do not come to terms with the interior call which is given to them.

It was in suffering that the Lord himself spoke to us. And in suffering he takes up his abode with us, so that the mystery of his being takes flesh in us. Sorrow builds a bridge into the infinite and becomes the meetingplace of God and man. Suffering without faith is meaningless, and faith without suffering cannot be in this world. Sometimes, as things get harder on the outside, they become easier within.

Your love gives me being

Beloved,

Your letter reached me at a time when I was very low, but the love that came with it lifted me up. It gave me the hind's feet to climb the mountain again. You have let me share in the divine love which you have embodied for me. Your word is a kind of enfleshment of the Word ofGod.

Most of us poor humans are wandering the world in search of someone to fall in love with us. From what you tell me, there was something more God-like in your own journey. You were seeking not so much to be loved, as reaching out into the darkness to bring the light of love to another. It is that radiance that has lightened my darkness. There seems to be an energy that has caught fire from the eternal flame of love in the way you have come into my life. In you, the divine flame and the human spark seem to be fused. The philosophers would call it the divine information of being.

When I pray to God, your presence is never far away, for I find you in all the pathways to heaven and you walk beside me. To the Lord of glory and to your dear self, I seem to make the one prayer: 'You are my all, my everything. Without you, I am nothing. Your creative love gives me being. In you I live and have my being.'

I like what you have written, about the relationship which is at the heart ofthe Blessed Trinity. And that it takes a trinity to love – you, me and God who is Divine Trinity. Our longing for each other is a yearning for the streams of living water that flow from the hills of heaven to make green our valley.

Prayer for Divine Love

Most Blessed Trinity grant your holy wisdom
to men and women, celibate and married,
that they may seek to love,
through the Divine Humanity of Jesus.
Through the burning love of his Heart,
through his sacred wounds,
pour light into our souls
so that all may understand
that lasting love
and its true enjoyment
is only possible
through Jesus, the Reconciler.
Mary, Immaculate, Queen of the Universe,
Mother of God, be with us in our love.
O Divine Humanity,
I crave for the church
and for the world
an understanding
of thy unique, beautiful
and all satisfying love.
O heal the wounds of sin carried by the
children of men for so long.
O rhythm of Divine Love,
pulsate through all creation
So that we may reach that fulness of love
for which you minutely designed us.
O good God, let us enjoy you and each other
in the harmony of your love.
Pulsating love of our Trinitarian God,
Sweep mightily
through your expectant creation.